A Royal Priesthood

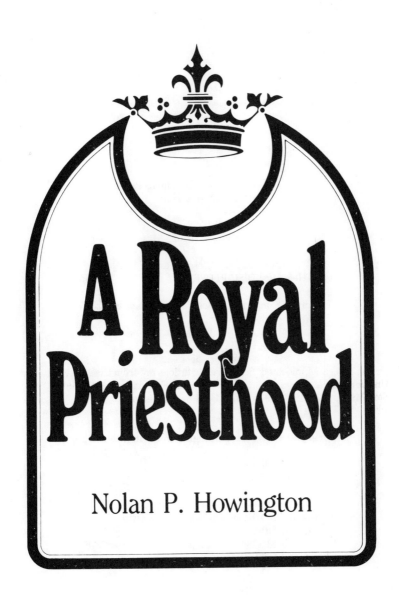

A Royal Priesthood

Nolan P. Howington

BROADMAN PRESS
Nashville, Tennessee

4216-22
ISBN: 0-8054-1622-6

Dewey Decimal Classification: 248.4
Subject Headings: DISCIPLESHIP // LAITY // CHURCH

Library of Congress Catalog Card Number: 85-22376

Printed in the United States of America

Unless otherwise indicated, Scripture quotations are from the *New American Standard Bible*. Copyright © The Lockman Foundation, 1960, 1962, 1963, 1968, 1971, 1972, 1973, 1975, 1977. Used by permission.

Library of Congress Cataloging-in-Publication Data

Howington, Nolan P.
 A royal priesthood.

 1. Christian life—Baptist authors. 2. Laity—
Baptists. 3. Priesthood, Universal. 4. Baptists—
Doctrines. I. Title.
BV4501.2.H618 1986   248.4′86132   85-22376
ISBN 0-8054-1622-6 (pbk.)

Contents

1

New Eyes for Old

Acts 9:18

No single conversion experience is a pattern for all others. Some conversions are sudden and emotional; others are gradual and free of emotional upheaval. But every authentic conversion produces change and attests the power of God to alter human nature.

A well-established piece of evidence, we are told, always outweighs the negative. The conversion experience of Saul of Tarsus is therefore proof positive that God is able to transform persons. The life that followed Paul's encounter with Christ confirms the validity of the experience.

You need only to survey the achievements of this Pharisee turned Christian. He traveled extensively, boldly proclaiming his faith. He bridged the gap between Jew and Gentile, established and strengthened churches, wrote epistles, corrected doctrinal errors, developed Christian theology, and gave Christianity standing within the Roman world.

This all started one day when God confronted a fanatical Pharisee ten miles southwest of Damascus. Bent on crushing Judaism's rival, Saul encountered the Head of the new movement. Saul came away blinded and shaken to the core of his being. Days later as the Christian Ananias ministered to him, he regained his sight. The film over his eyes was peeled back as one removes bark from a sapling. God gave him new eyes for the old.

The Replacement of the Old with Something New

Those falling scales suggest *the replacement of the old with something new.* Paul's life was radically changed. This transformation, as he would later say, was like shedding dirty, old garments for new ones.

His Beastly Nature Was Changed

For one thing, *his beastly nature was changed*. Luke describes a man thoroughly dedicated to the destruction of the church and Christians. Like a fierce dragon "breathing threats and murder" (Acts 9:1), he assaulted the followers of Christ. The death of Stephen had whetted his appetite for blood. Now he turned with fanatical zeal to wipe out all the Christians. Later, he painfully recalled his actions as devastating, like a conqueror sacking a city (Gal. 1:13).

The dark side of human nature assumes various forms. The beast in us may take the shape of a cunning jackal or a ludicrous monkey. Sometimes it is the dumbness of an ox, the stupidity of an ass, the fierceness of a tiger, or the pride of a peacock. The beast is never so beastly as when it hides beneath a religious form. One of the strangest facts of history is the brutality of religious persons toward those who oppose them. Can we ever forget that the religious establishment pushed vigorously for Jesus' death until He was fastened to a cross?

The beastly nature must be changed, not just curbed momentarily. But how changed? Paul (his Roman name) had diligently sought to please God through a rigid obedience to the law. He had found therein only futility and despair. Then Paul met a deliverer (Rom. 7:25), and found a freedom he had never before known (Rom. 8:2). Human nature, even for the "chief of sinners," could be radically altered. And it is like getting new eyes for old.

The Change Was a Miracle of Grace

This obviously is *a miracle of grace*. But there are certain factors at work in this man's life. As Adolf Deissmann notes, "The lightning of Damascus strikes no empty space but finds deep in the soul of the persecutor plenty of inflammable material."[1] There was Paul's own sense of despair over his inability to meet the demands of the law. Was he also troubled by his ruthless treatment of the Christians and the courageous manner they met imprisonment and death? Possibly he remembered the tolerant Gamaliel's caution against resisting God (Acts 5:34-39). Could the Christians be right, and might he not be fighting God?

Then there was the memory of Stephen's death. He had voted to kill a man whose testimony for Christ could not be answered by logic nor silenced by force. Though he had hurled no stones, he had sanctioned the killing of that Christian man. Stephen's bloody face upturned toward heaven was etched in Paul's memory. He kept hearing the dying man's prayer, "Lord Jesus, receive my spirit! . . . Do not hold this sin against them!" (Acts 7:59-60). Who but a righteous man could pray like that? Later, Augustine was to remark, "If Stephen had not so prayed, the church would not have Paul today." Persons do not meet death for a worthless idea or for love of a phony messiah. Thus the Spirit used a martyr's death to disturb a crusading fanatic.

God also used natural phenomena in Saul's conversion. There was the dusty road, a sultry noontide, and a beating sun. Suddenly, the traveler saw a blinding flash, like unexpected lightning, and heard a thunderous boom. Blinded, he fell to the earth. A voice asked, "Saul, Saul, why are you persecuting Me?" (Acts 9:4). For in hounding the churches the raving man had indeed been battling against God.

Martin Luther, who loved Paul's freedom letter, Galatians, also had a dramatic conversion experience. His soul had been stirred by his study of the Latin Bible and by a sickness which had almost destroyed him. He was traveling with his friend Alexis through the Thuringian Forest. A terrific electrical storm broke about them. A bolt of lightning killed Alexis and tore up the ground at Luther's feet. He felt that the Day of Wrath had come and "compassed with terror and the agony of death," he devoted himself to God from that hour. Inward peace, however, came only after years of struggle when he found that salvation comes by faith (Rom. 1:17), not by works.[2] Like Paul, Luther emerged from bondage a free man. He received new eyes for old.

New Eyes See Things in a Different Light

The reality of divine power meets the reality of our sin and we are made new creatures. That brings clear vision.

New Eyes See Jesus Aright

The One whom Paul had viewed as an impostor he now saw as Savior and Friend. From a despised Nazarene, a repugnant teacher of heretical doctrine, Jesus was now the authoritative Lord of truth. To regenerate minds, Jesus Christ is always different. Personal faith brings a sense of certitude concerning Him. The smartest person, who seeks to belittle following Jesus, is a poor match for the simplest person who has a convincing faith in Jesus.

For many of us Jesus has come alive as He did for Paul. From a promise on a page, we now know Him as a personal Redeemer. Instead of an abstract principle in theology, He is for us a living presence. Once a mere historical figure, He is now a trusted friend.

Can a person so changed be silent about his newfound faith? Paul could not. Immediately he began to tell people what had happened to him. His hearers were amazed, then suspicious, then convinced that God had indeed turned him around.

Out of our confidence in Christ and our experience of love, we are motivated to witness and to minister. Here, too, is the highest motive for right conduct. All things change with His entry into our lives.

New Eyes See Sin in a Different Light

Sin is a condition of our soul, not a mere infraction of law. It is an ugly, repulsive disease rather than a small sore easily treated. Sin is the disposition to repudiate love, to live apart from God. The biblical revelation declares the possibilities of human beings but never lets us forget the devastating results of iniquity.

George Buttrick once described the naivete of two college girls who were discussing his lecture on the atonement. "He kept talking about sin," one remarked. "What did he mean?"

The other replied, "Oh, that has something to do with Adam and Eve!"[3] It also has something to do with us!

Human nature, untouched by divine grace, runs afoul of God's purposes and rushes headlong toward perdition. Sin snaps off the light of judgment, distorts conscience, weakens the will, and guides the individual toward destruction. Sin also harasses the Christian who must rely fully upon Christ's power lest evil mar the fellowship with the Master. Paul hated his past sins, lived guardedly due to recurring temptation, and rejoiced endlessly because of God's strong hand upon his life. Like him, proximity to Christ keeps us increasingly sensitive to sin and secure against its dominion.

New Eyes See People in a Different Light

The controlling love of Christ opens our eyes to the essential worth of persons. "From now on we recognize no man according to the flesh" (2 Cor. 5:16). Each person becomes a brother for whom Christ died (1 Cor. 8:11). This criterion of worth challenges the abuse or misuse of persons. It forbids that we ignore individuals, for thereby we call in question their inherent value as persons created in God's image. We who have been rescued by a great love must reflect that love in all personal relationships.

This is true even when the other person has a different skin color, social classification, or national background. The converted life, one oriented around Christ, must look at people through His eyes. Granting every person one's place and rights for some of us represents a step forward. But Christ in us requires that we accept and treat lovingly every person we meet. He Who tore down the dividing walls wills one humanity (Eph. 2:14-16). Nothing else satisfies Him.

Did you ever see an old-fashioned patchwork quilt? In our farm home, our mother used to make two or three quilts each year. Then Mother would bring out of her treasures the variously colored scraps she had been gathering all year. Then she cut them into a pattern and laboriously sewed them together. The quilting frame was then suspended from the ceiling. Across the frame she would place a large sheet of cloth and cover it with a layer of cotton. Then the sheet of colored scraps that had been sewn together was placed over the layer of cotton. After that came the tedious stitching through the layers of cloth and cotton. The finished product would look the same on one side, but the topside would be a patchwork of colors.

Our nation is much like that quilt. In our basic humanity we are one, sharing great similarities. The racial or ethnic distinctives are the separate pieces highlighting our differences. All are woven together into a pattern of democratic life. Even more, we are one through Him who has broken down the "wall of partition." The new mind-set helps us to accept one another, for distinctions are meaningless. "Christ is all, and in all" (Col. 3:11).

New Eyes View the Church in a Different Light

No one who is a friend of Jesus Christ can be hostile toward the church, His body. The man who sought to destroy the church and the memory of its Founder became an apostle for Christ and a founder of churches. In finding Christ he found the church. God's judgment may rest upon the church, as Peter recognized (1 Pet. 4:17). But it is His purpose to disclose His manifold wisdom through the church (Eph. 3:10). Though never without "spot or wrinkle" (Eph. 5:27), the church nonetheless is God's creation and no person who claims to be in Christ can refuse to accept one's place within the body of Christ.

Membership in that body admits us to a redemptive fellowship within which we find nurture and strength. But like Paul, we also find there our ministry for the Master. For the natural consequence of conversion is a share in that ministry directed by the Spirit and sanctioned by fellow believers (Acts 13:1-4). Selfish souls may seek a given church for what they can get out of it. Sincere Christians seek a church that helps them become increasingly useful for Christ. The institutional church is one means whereby disciples of Christ honor the One about whom their lives revolve.

Christ Brings Joy to Our Lives

There is joy in the sight and insight that Christ brings to our lives. There is also joy in helping another find new eyes for old. A couple with two small boys discovered that the younger lad had problems with mobility. He stumbled about, falling over objects in his path, and could not fit into play patterns with other children. The parents had the child examined by several specialists before one found the trouble. The little fellow had been born with progressive myopia. The doctor fitted him with thick-lens glasses, and for the first time the child saw clearly. He came into a new world of colors, beautiful objects, and the faces of family members. Everywhere he turned, interesting experiences awaited him. He began to live anew when he began to see.

It is that way with a person who has found the Savior and the new life He gives. Never mind if your experience differs from Saul of Tarsus or the neighbor next door. Make sure of this, "One thing I do know, that whereas I was blind, now I see" (John 9:25).

2

Testing
for Discipleship

Mark 10:21

The Book of Mark, says Eduard Schweizer, "resembles a volume of sermons more than a biography."[1] If that is true, then the message found in Mark 10:17-31 might be entitled "Testing for Discipleship."

Jesus and a wealthy young ruler met one day around an urgent question, "What shall I do to inherit eternal life?" That young man was concerned literally with eternal life, life in God's presence beyond physical death. A question like that opens the door for the evangelist to give his best answer and his strongest appeal.

What did Jesus do? Mark tells us that Jesus loved the man. Surely He desired to enlist him as a disciple. W. O. Carver believed that Jesus could have made this man an apostle like Saul of Tarsus. He possessed many credentials for such a role.

Jesus, however, moved like a person who wanted to lose a follower! He offered no soft approach to discipleship. Never once, so far as I know, did He lower the gospel's demands in order to get a following. His whole demeanor is a corrective for any superficial evangelism that sweeps persons into the church without confronting them with the high standards of God's kingdom.

Holiness Brings Awareness of Sin

With good reason, Jesus directed the prospective disciple toward God Himself. For the sense of a holy God provokes in us an awareness of sin. "There is none good but . . . God" (Mark 10:18, KJV). His goodness shows up our badness. In contrast to His holiness, our righteousness is like filthy rags (Isa. 64:6).

Before His moral perfection we can only cry, "Woe is me, for I am ruined! Because I am a man of unclean lips, and I live among a people of unclean lips, For my eyes have seen the King, the Lord of hosts" (Isa. 6:5).

Jesus challenged the glib ascription of goodness to persons, even to Himself. He did not disclaim His own personal goodness, but He did turn the young man's attention toward the One who alone is perfect goodness. Before the holy God, neither men nor angels are pure (Job 4:18; 15:15; 25:3 f). Being human, Jesus was identified with sinners and experienced temptation. This cannot be said of God. Though Jesus claimed to be one with God, He pointed away from Himself to the Father. "The Father is greater than I" (John 14:28).

Admittedly, in Jesus of Nazareth we have our fullest revelation of God. But God cannot be wholly contained within any human form. Jesus seems to say that God is greater than any revelation of Himself. God cannot be confined to the church, the Bible, or even the human life of Jesus. He is Spirit (John 4:24), perfectly free, disclosing Himself as He wills, but always more than our minds can know. Jesus brings God close to us in mercy and love. Our relation to Him is that of children with a gracious Father. But He is not One to be manipulated, nor is He a cheap deity with whom we can become chummy. Over-familiarity toward God can be the opposite of that reverence which persons should feel in His presence.

The sense of a holy God drives the wedge of guilt into our souls. Small wonder that the world tries so hard to bury God under a blanket of denial and repudiation or reduce His size through mutilated and distorted theologies. We find it hard to face the God of glory, so we try through every means to cut Him down to fit our patterns of thought and life. Will Herberg, Jewish social philosopher, feels that modern man is attempting something new, the full removal of God and His laws from life. People, he says, have always ignored or disobeyed the divine law but have lived with guilt and uncertainty as a result. In our time, however, persons are trying to free themselves of God altogether. If that can be done, then one can dismiss guilt and responsibility. This can never be accomplished. It is a mark of human pride and arrogance even to attempt it.

The beginning point for any worthy evangelistic appeal is the awareness of a holy God whom we must face, whose word we must hear, whose righteousness we had better accept. And Jesus made it. As I recall vividly, it was this sense of God, following me like a "hound of heaven," producing in me an intolerable guilt, that led to my conversion. A God-consciousness precedes a sin-consciousness.

External Acts Never Correct the Moral Bankruptcy of Our Souls

Jesus confronted the young ruler with a second fact. External acts never correct the moral bankruptcy of our souls. The moral law of God expressed in commandments imposes an ideal which eludes unregenerate persons. Indeed, the Commandments may frustrate us, for they declare the nature of our sin without giving us power to master it (Rom. 7:7-23). There is a fallacy in the question, What shall I do to inherit eternal life? Eternal life comes by gift, not by human deeds.

Why, then, does Jesus bring the Commandments to the young ruler's attention? Because Jesus took them seriously. He distinguished between ritual practice and moral law. One is temporary; the other, timeless. The Commandments express the mind of God. They rise out of His righteous will and reveal His moral character. They form the basis for orderly and stable community life. Taken together, they call for a reverence for God, a respect for human life and property, a fidelity to sexual standards and family patterns, a devotion to truthfulness and honesty in personal relationships.

Will you notice that Jesus used the expression, "Do not defraud"? The verb that is used sometimes referred to withholding hired workers' wages or failure to return goods or money at the appropriate time. Had the man been guilty of unjust dealings? Whatever Jesus meant to convey, the man seemed to lack security and happiness. The law had not produced these. His wealth and achievements brought no peace.

Before God, our external acts are inadequate unless they flow out of a life that has been renewed within. Jesus felt a deep compassion for the clean, morally upright man. He saw his sincerity and moral earnestness. He wanted to help him find the answer to his question.

The righteousness which Christ teaches is *inward,* not external. It belongs to that life which has been made over again, a life under His control, a life with a new mind and a new set of priorities. The most morally bankrupt life or the most self-righteous, good person can be rescued from self-centeredness and made new. That is what happened to a young nurse who came under the influence of Christian companions. She had never known a normal family life. Her parents were theatrical performers who had little time for their daughter, and even less for God. Her first exposure to Christ came when she entered nurse's training. She hungered for that serenity and sense of purpose which she saw in her new friends. This interest led her to join them on a weekend retreat where she made a decision for Christ. Later she was trying to describe what took place. Said she, "I can't put it in words, but it was something like being born." She had stumbled onto Jesus' own description of the experience of conversion.

What do we bring to this kind of experience? Nothing but an open, penitent heart. We come to God in the spirit of little children who have nothing going for them but their helplessness and need (Mark 10:14). Before Him, we can make no claims for ourselves or press any demands upon Him. We are bankrupt, like a Zacchaeus or a Mary Magdalene.

> In my hand no price I bring,
> Simply to Thy cross I cling.

> —AUGUSTUS M. TOPLADY

The Call to Discipleship Involves Renunciation

Jesus' words, "One thing you lack," fell like a bomb across the consciousness of the morally upright man. You see, he did have lots of things going for him. He showed courage in coming to Jesus in broad daylight. Respect for a great leader caused him to fall down humbly before Him. His sincerity and eagerness were quite evident. And he felt honestly that he had a good track record in keeping the Commandments.

With characteristic insight Jesus spoke to the young man's real problem. He was a self-centered person whose life was dominated by his wealth. The possession of goods was not in itself evil, but it had come to be a barrier between him and God. The perils of wealth are real, but so are complacency, selfish ambition, self-will, pride, and bitterness. In dealing with us, Christ calls on us to surrender whatever constitutes a barrier between us and God.

Jesus' radical demand startled this man. It also shook the disciples, who probably viewed the man's riches as a sure sign of divine favor. We can understand the young man's dilemma. After all, Jesus' identity as Son of God and authoritative Lord had not yet been established. The cross and the resurrection were future events. Even Jesus' immediate followers were not clear about His identity and mission. To this man, Jesus was a notable teacher, perhaps a great prophet. Hence Jesus' sharp demand for total renunciation disturbed that man's soul. "Go and sell all you possess, and give it to the poor, and you shall have treasure in heaven." To act upon such a challenge called for faith in the person of Jesus and an acceptance of His authority.

Jesus, you see, was challenging accepted patterns of success and the theological view that prosperity and wealth accompanied by power, were signs of divine favor. He who was soon to die upon a cross resisted this prevailing view. What can we say about our own easy and secure life, our inordinate worship of mammon and self, our insulation from the poor whom God loves so devotedly? Could we *hear,* much less translate into action, Jesus' call to renounce all that we *are* and all that we *have?* The test of discipleship can be hard indeed.

Jesus hardly meant that one can buy one's way into the kingdom of God. No, He is saying that the essential self which we are must be totally surrendered to Him, to all that He demands of us. "Treasure in heaven" is a Jewish term. It really means the things that God counts significant, in contrast to life's false securities and transitory goods.[2] What Jesus seeks is a new person whose center now is Christ, not self or the things that reflect a self-centered self.

Discipleship Calls for a Total Commitment to Christ

This call for a total commitment is expressed in three simple words, "Come, follow me" (v. 21). Those words mean far more than a change of vocation, though for some they may require that. Jesus' invitation here is similar to the one issued to His first disciples (Mark 1:17; 2:14). It was the common expression used by any great teacher who wished to enlist a following. The invitation could thus mean leaving all to follow after a Master. "Forsaking all" could involve giving up a cherished position, a family relationship, or one's ambitious goals (Luke 9:23; 14:25-33). Whether or not such action results, the disciple must be open to the possibility and willing to carry it out if obedience to Christ takes that shape.

Jesus' invitation is to a full-orbed discipleship. That is not restricted to the small group who serve as pastors, teachers, missionaries, and church staff persons. Discipleship means setting Christ first in life, giving Him the place of primacy in everything. All else must come beneath that solid commitment to Him. That holds true whether we continue our present vocation and location or leave these for other places and other forms of service.

Christ is unquestionably Lord of our lives. Every decision we make and every direction we take must reflect that fact. Even the thoughts of our minds are to become "captive to the obedience of Christ" (2 Cor. 10:5).

There is a continuity about the disciple's commitment. It is not given, then withdrawn. The ways it is expressed may change, but the essential commitment is for life. Once in a conference on Christian doctrine, the discussion came to dwell upon the relation between being "in Christ" and being in the church. How significant is membership in the body of Christ? One thoughtful person asked, "How do you account for the fact that some church members live like pagans? They have no loyalty to their church, their life-styles are not Christian, they give little evidence of ever having been saved." That is a disturbing observation, with no easy answer.

Jesus' words, "You will know them by their fruits" (Matt. 7:20), are applicable here. Good fruits indicate a sound, healthy tree. Another response to that conferee's problem is to study the lives of God's faithful children. They provide convincing proof of God's power and presence. This company of the committed fortify our souls and encourage us to remain true to our Lord.

Christ's call to total commitment can be as offensive to our ears as it was to the rich young ruler's. It is enough to frighten away any superficial inquirer. Jesus did not lower His demand in order to gain a follower. Would we have made the way easier for that young man? What church would not welcome such a potential leader, an energetic and well-trained person, a wealthy man who might soon become a treasurer or a major contributor? We probably allow individuals to enter the church with fewer qualities than this man possessed. In so doing, we fail them, for they may still lack one thing, the most important thing, Jesus Christ as Lord and Savior of the life.

A person may fail the test of discipleship. This man did. He went away reluctantly, grieved in spirit (v. 22). But he did go away. Jesus had other hearers to walk away from Him (John 6:66), but this man is singled out in the Gospels as one who openly rejected Jesus' command to follow Him. He put tangible values, perishable goods like wealth, success, and acclaim, above the joy of membership in God's family. What more can be done for a person who puts such trifles above the gift of eternal life? And in refusing to meet Christ's terms, the individual's initial grief may be the beginning of an even greater sorrow.

Should not our evangelistic appeals be as fair and honest as the one issued by Jesus? There can be no legitimate obscuring of Jesus' stringent demands. From the onset of the believer's conversion, one is under the lordship of Christ. Each of us is called to lifelong discipleship. Persons who come with open eyes into the Christian life, knowing the requirements in advance and accepting them willingly, make loyal disciples and functioning church members. Of such is the kingdom of heaven!

3

The Model
for Ministry

Hebrews 2:17-18

There are restaurants that sometimes include a style show with its luncheon hour. Attractive ladies parade across a platform and through the dining area, pausing by each table to let patrons see the lovely garments being modeled. The model's function is to show off the dresses. If beauty of face and form enhance beauty of fabric, that is most welcome.

Models are everywhere. The word itself is commonplace. There are model houses, model programs, model machines, model parents, model teachers, and model schools. Webster defines a *model* as "a person or thing considered as a standard of excellence to be imitated." The model may be useful for inspiring or enforcing conduct. From childhood we have been enjoined to emulate certain patterns of behavior, adopt select values, and follow the example of worthy persons. Whether so enjoined or not, most of us have our heroes, our human idols such as ministers, athletes, actors, militarists, or musicians. We ape their mannerisms, adopt their life-styles, and defend their moral miscues.

Models can let us down mighty hard. The athlete we adore turns to drugs or gambling; the musician or actor gets hooked on alcohol and drugs or proves to be horribly self-centered; the stars that dazzle us may also disappoint us. In sharp contrast are the godly persons who minister to our need for guidance and moral example. Of those quite naturally is One who stands tall and true and unchanging. Biblical writers lift Him up as the Model *par excellence* whose life we may imitate without fear of being let down. Obviously, Jesus is far more than an example; He is a Savior to be loved and a Master to be obeyed.

Even so, He is eminently worthy of imitation. This is especially true concerning the ministry each of us is called to perform. In what sense is His ministry a model for ours?

Authentic Ministry Calls for an Identity with Persons

"He had to be made like His brethren in all things, that He might become a merciful and faithful high priest" (Heb. 2:17). Jesus shared our "flesh and blood" existence (v. 14). He partook of human nature in its fullness. The incarnation, God's unique revelation in a human life, is a profound mystery. How can the Almighty God become man? "The Word became flesh and dwelt among us," so John declared (1:14). The testimony of Matthew and Luke is that He entered the human family through a miraculous birth. According to Paul, "God sent forth His Son, born of a woman" (Gal. 4:4). The incarnation was God's idea. Neither Jew nor Greek thought up that one.

The reality of Jesus' manhood cannot be questioned or set aside. The denial of His humanity is as fatal to New Testament faith as is the denial of His deity.[1] The biblical writers wrestled with the mystery of the incarnation but they surrendered neither His deity nor His humanity. In fact, they labored mightily to convince the world that Jesus—the earthly Jesus—was indeed the Son of God. In our own day, the reverse is often true. People tend to overlook Jesus' humanity or view Him as a superhuman.

Identity with flesh-and-blood people rather than angels equipped Jesus to minister helpfully to "the seed of Abraham" (Heb. 2:16, KJV). Out of that relationship with men and women, He acquired understanding and sympathy, two indispensable qualities for ministry. These developed out of His experience with temptation, suffering, and death. Each aspect of that experience was genuine. Jesus fought no mock battles. He was "tempted in all things as we are, yet without sin" (Heb. 4:15). One who quickly succumbs to temptation never knows how intense that temptation can become. Jesus felt the full pressure of temptation, but He never yielded to its power. That experience equipped Him to minister with deeper sympathy and understanding.

No person's ministry to others requires that He Himself have firsthand experience of evil. One needs no third-degree burns to warn another of fire. The mastery of evil puts us in a better position to help persons than experimentation with various forms of sin.

Were the sufferings of Jesus real? If we can believe the unanimous testimony of Scripture, they were. In fact, His suffering itself presented a source of temptation (Heb. 2:18). Did He feel depression, loneliness of spirit, or bitter despair because of the things He endured? And in death, was not His lament "My God, My God, why hast Thou forsaken Me?" (Mark 15:34) indicative of that despair? He tasted of death, drinking its bitter dregs. This was more than physical death (1 John 3:14). It was His conquest of the realm of death over which Satan reigned. We are thereby set free of the terror and sting of death (Heb. 2:14-15). This glorious truth needs to be proclaimed for all people to hear. That surely is a part of the ministry Jesus grants us to perform.

Jesus launched His ministry from the platform of His incarnation. Look at His way of helping people. He never stood at a distance from persons, content to send them prescriptions for their ills. It was His practice to rub shoulders with them, sometimes touching them as He did the leper (Mark 1:41) to establish an identity with them. He had an amazing insight into human nature, especially disturbed minds and disrupted lives. His heart went out to diseased persons, small and great alike. The bulk of His miracles were performed on behalf of such persons.

Those of us who would serve people in His name must find ways as He did to identify with persons. His agenda for ministry must become ours (Luke 4:18-20; 7:22-23). Nor is this a task only for trained, skilled performers. All God's people are called to ministry, and multitudes of plain, ordinary church members regularly give cups of cold water in Christ's name (Mark 9:41).

Effective Ministry Is Characterized by Self-Giving

Effective ministry is characterized by self-giving, even to the point of suffering. This, so the Book of Hebrews declares, was true of Jesus. As our High Priest, He makes one offering for us, the offering of Himself. He becomes the "propitiation for the sins of the people" (2:17), the "once for all" sacrifice made in our behalf (7:27; 9:28; 10:10). His offering was both voluntary and vicarious. Through it, He did something that had never been done before, something that never had to be repeated. Sacrificial, self-giving love broke the back of sin and liberated us from its paralyzing power. "He died for all," wrote Paul, "that they who live should no longer live for themselves, but for Him who died and rose again on their behalf" (2 Cor. 5:15). God made Christ "who knew no sin to be sin in our behalf that we might become the righteousness of God in Him" (v. 21).

Furthermore, "God was in Christ, reconciling the world to Himself" (2 Cor. 5:19). Fisher Humphreys calls this "cruciform forgiveness." God incarnate in Christ forgives us out of the pain and suffering of Christ. Divine forgiveness has taken a new shape, one that it will retain.[2] There is now a straight line to God. "Let us therefore draw near with confidence to the throne of grace, that we may receive mercy and may find grace to help in time of need" (Heb. 4:16). The confident approach to God, once limited to priests, is now open to all believers. Christ has made possible an easier access to God. He has also extended the privilege of ministry to each of us. That ministry draws on the resources of heaven. It must also share His spirit of sacrificial self-giving. Are we ready for that?

Challenges Our Self-Centeredness

First of all, that kind of ministry to human need challenges our self-centeredness. We are influenced by the popular view that the world owes us a living, that we should be on the receiving end, that others should serve our interests. Yet the pattern of Jesus is just the opposite. "For even the Son of Man did not come to be served, but to serve, and to give His life a ransom for many" (Mark 10:45). That statement flies in the teeth of our self-interest.

Requires Expenditures of Time, Resources, and Self

Second, a self-giving ministry requires expenditures of time, resources, and self. Ministry is not an ideal designed only for discussion in small groups. It is kneeling by the roadside, touching the dirty, bloody victim of brigands, and doing what is required to help him (Luke 10:33-35). Ministry is spending time with lonely persons in convalescent homes or disturbed persons in broken families. It is surrendering the ease and comfort of home to share hours with grief-stricken or guilt-laden persons. Ministry has many forms, but all of them demand time and the giving of self.

May Call for Some Suffering

Third, ministry may call for some suffering. To enter the lives of persons and to take on their burdens is an act of love. But it can lead to pain as we empathize with those we seek to help. Ministering spirits often run into hostile persons or dangerous situations. Even apart from this, there is a frightful drain on our emotional energies as we fulfill our ministries. We soon learn to rely upon the power and insight that God provides. We work out of our humanity, for only thus can we help persons, but we desperately need the strength that God provides.

We Minister in Things Pertaining to God

Fourth, we minister to flesh-and-blood people, but we minister "in things pertaining to God" (Heb. 2:17). Without apology we seek to bring persons to know Him and to align their lives with His purposes for them. You and I may be God's instruments to bring consolation, encouragement, hope, and love to others. Ultimately, however, the focus must shift from us to the Source which fortifies and undergirds and redeems individuals. Jesus Himself did that during His ministry.

Some of the world's noblest souls have exemplified the self-giving kind of ministry found in Jesus. Albert Schweitzer was such an example. A competent scholar, gifted musician, pastor, and trained surgeon, he turned his back on a promising career in Germany. He planted his life and devoted his energies to service as a missionary surgeon in French Equatorial Africa. A brilliant Japanese scholar, Toyohiko Kagawa, caught from Christ a vision of ministry and poured out his life amid the poor and downtrodden masses in Japan. Amid all the honors and acclaim he received, he maintained his identity with the poor. For multitudes, this man reflected the sacrificial, self-giving spirit of Jesus. In more recent years, William Wallace, Baptist medical missionary to China, gave himself tirelessly in ministry far removed from his native Tennessee. He died in prison at Communist hands.

Lives of great men and women stir us by their selfless devotion to Christ. Such persons seem to belong in a world removed from our plain existence. But look around you. You will find ordinary individuals like yourself serving with the mind and attitude of Christ in all kinds of ways and places. There are dedicated souls who love children and have devoted a significant part of their lives teaching and training minds. Patient and sympathetic adults work with youth and become their example and source of guidance in a confused world. Businessmen and businesswomen may work in downtown missions, perform services in hospitals and homes for the elderly. Sensitive persons take the spirit of Jesus with them into their daily vocations with never an apology for doing so. Professional people, guided by the vision of human need, go in Christ's name to earth's troubled spots to minister in medicine, dentistry, agriculture, carpentry, teaching, and other areas. Often this is done at their own expense.

Authentic Ministry Means Intercession

Jesus is our prime example of effective intercession. In the broader sense, intercession means action in behalf of another person. It can be a form of pleading, like a mother I once heard interceding eloquently for her son before a judge in juvenile court. Or it can be seen in a rural pastor urging his people to help a struggling preacher boy who lacks money to handle college expenses. Seen in this light, the whole ministry of Jesus is a form of intercession. Our emphasis here, however, will be on intercessory prayer. This is a vital ministry open to all persons.

The Book of Hebrews graphically describes Jesus' prayer life. "In the days of His flesh, He offered up both prayers and supplications with loud crying and tears to the One able to save Him from death, and He was heard because of His piety. Although He was a Son, He learned obedience from the things which He suffered" (5:7-8). It is understandable when one makes intercession for Himself as Jesus did in Gethsemane. For profound grief, literally horror and dismay, pressed down upon His soul (Mark 14:33-36). He prayed for the removal of the cup of suffering and death, but it remained. Do we need help when we are faced with the mystery and trial of unanswered prayer? Certainly we need, as He did, special grace to drink the cup when it remains.

The Son learned obedience within the context of suffering. Otherwise, He would not have been able to intercede for us. However, the truth is that "He is able to save forever those who draw near to God through Him, since He always lives to make intercession for us" (Heb. 7:25). Critics who discount prayer in general may play down the place of intercession. But intercession was the whole thrust of Jesus' life. As Moses stood between God and Israel (Ex. 32:32), so Jesus stands between humanity and the Father.

Intercession is bringing the needs of persons to God's attention. Even though He knows beforehand what individuals need (Matt. 6:32), we are enjoined to pray for them. Does not God realize the shortage of workers in the Kingdom? Assuredly, but Jesus asks His followers to pray to God for helpers in the harvest fields (Matt. 9:38; Luke 10:2). Jesus prayed for His disciples and for future generations of followers (John 17:9-11,15,20-24). This is enough to encourage our intercessions and to give validity to them.

Even now, Jesus carries on a ministry of intercession (Heb. 7:25; Rom. 8:34). He is the mediator between God and human beings (1 Tim. 2:5). Because He uniquely combines Godhead and manhood in His own person, He is perfectly equipped for this work. "In Him God draws near to men and in Him men draw near to God, with the assurance of constant and immediate access."[3] It is a comfort to know that the living Christ maintains His sympathy and carries on a ministry of intercession for His struggling people here on earth. And for some reason He invites us to share that ministry.

Testimonies to the effectiveness of intercession are more convincing than arguments for or against its validity. James supported his appeal for intercessory prayer by the statement, "The effective prayer of a righteous man can accomplish much" (Jas. 5:16). Then he cited Elijah as an example (5:17-18). Augustine's saintly mother, Monica, prayed fervently for her son. God laid hold of Augustine because she had so mightily laid hold of God.

A public-school teacher once shared her concern for her wayward brother. He had broken away from the religious influences of the family. She and her sisters regularly prayed for him. Said she, "We have not troubled Mother with his behavior. Should we continue to shelter her? For you know no one can pray for a wayward son or daughter like a Christian mother."

Prayer is not a substitute for work or witnessing. But our best efforts in themselves are not good enough. We are impelled to pray for God's help both for ourselves and the persons we would help. When intercession is done in His name and in His Spirit, it affects the flow of divine resources. How this is accomplished is a mystery. But too many persons have tested its reality for us glibly to turn aside from it. Because of intercessory prayer, many burdens are lifted or made bearable. New impulses, new insights, and fresh energies come through the prayers of devoted friends. Take seriously the ministry of intercession!

> The day was long, the burden I had borne
> Seemed heavier than I could longer bear,
> And then it lifted—but I did not know
> Some one had knelt in prayer.[4]

Jesus is one model we can follow without fear that He will ever let us down. His way of doing ministry remains the pattern for our own. His agenda is still ours to follow. This is true for the church and for the individual alike. We owe it to Jesus that He not only opens up the way to God, but He grants to all believers a share in His ministry.

4

The Royal Priesthood

1 Peter 2:4-10

As our plane approached the Nashville airport, it hovered briefly over Percy Priest Lake. Beneath us lay the main body of water with innumerable small coves. Each cove was related to the lake as fingers are related to a hand. But no small finger of water could claim to be the whole body.

In some ways the doctrine of the priesthood of all believers resembles that lake with its inlets. The main body of water represents the basic doctrine and the inlets stand for truths related to it. To limit the doctrine to any one of its parts is a grave error. It overlooks the rich biblical rootage and the historical development of the doctrine.

Look at some of the attempts that have been made to define the priesthood of all believers: (1) Each Christian has access to God unaided by other persons save Christ alone. (2) Each believer has the right to interpret the Scripture for oneself. (3) Each believer is one's own authority in matters of faith and conduct. (4) Each believer has equal voting rights and privileges in a church assembly.[1] These are true statements, but they do not singly or together comprise the meaning of the doctrine.

In the biblical teaching about the royal priesthood, the focus is upon the church, not the individual. We tend to think of the individual, "the priesthood of the believer." There is merit in this, but Peter puts the emphasis upon the church in its corporate life. Thus the people of God share a common priesthood which is expressed in ministry under the lordship of Jesus Christ. Individual believers form a royal priesthood and are called to specific priestly service to one another and to the whole world.

The Royal Priesthood Is an Act of God

Peter uses the rich terminology of Exodus 19:5-6, language applied to Israel as God's chosen people. "If you will indeed obey My voice and keep My covenant, then you shall be My own possession among all the peoples, for all the earth is Mine; and you shall be to Me a kingdom of priests and a holy nation." These words point to all the people as priests, a nation under a great King. In token of this, the heads of families acted personally as priests in the yearly offering of the paschal lamb. A priestly class arose as representative of God's purpose for the nation. Israel seems never to have achieved God's intention among the nations. But God never abandoned that intention.

Intent on His redemptive mission, God raised up another community, a new Israel (Gal. 6:16) to bear witness to Him. The distinctive sign of this people, under a new covenant written on the heart, is baptism instead of circumcision. The new Israel's key memorial to God's grace and miraculous deliverance is the Lord's Supper with its symbols rather than the Passover meal. The God who guided Israel now guides the church and assigns to it a mission comparable to that once given Israel.

There is one profound difference between the old and the new Israel. Jesus Christ, the risen Lord, is mediator of the new and better covenant! He is a living reality in our experience. In Him God has been uniquely revealed. He has opened up the way to God for us (Heb. 4:16; 7:25). The church as a priestly community receives from Him its mediatorial task.

Dr. Theodore Adams, in a lecture on Christian preaching, described his ordination experience. His father delivered the charge to the young man in these words: "My son, stay close to God, stay close to people, and try to bring the two together." That is precisely what Christ, the Mediator between God and man, has done. It is also the work He gives us to do. In many ways, it is the main task of the priestly community, the church.

Our identity with Christ's death marks the beginning of life for us as believers. Our share in His resurrection equips us with power and makes us into a spiritual temple. "Coming to Him as to a living stone, rejected by men, but choice and precious in the sight of God, you also, as living stones, are being built up as a spiritual house for a holy priesthood" (1 Pet. 2:4-5).

In God's sight, each living stone is significant and possesses great worth. Each is a unique being responsible to God, coming voluntarily to relationship with Christ. Individually we are priests, accountable to God for the way we handle life with its opportunities. But a stone by itself does not constitute the spiritual temple of which Peter speaks. Its value is enhanced by union with other stones. The function of a stone is not to stand alone but to be joined to others in the formation of a "house."

There is no warrant in the New Testament for believing a person can be "in Christ" without at the same time being in the body of Christ. That heavy emphasis on individualism, characteristic of American culture and Christianity, has caused us to minimize the biblical teaching concerning solidarity and corporateness. The body of Christ has many parts, but it is one body. That body functions best when its parts are "fitted together" and each part is properly working to ensure growth (Eph. 2:19-22; 4:16).

This is the spiritual house in which God is pleased to dwell (1 Pet. 2:4-5; Eph. 2:21). Did not Jesus say, "Where two or three have gathered together in My name, there am I in their midst" (Matt. 18:20)? This is not a text designed to comfort us when church attendance is low but a promise that believers, gathered in Jesus' name, can count on His presence. He dwells among the people He has chosen for His own possession.

The church is an act of God, and He is the center of its life. This is evident in the descriptive terms Peter used to describe the church's worth (1 Pet. 2:9). Peter's "sermon" on the nature of the church, perhaps often preached, contains four points:

1. The church is a chosen race, God's choice of a people for His redemptive witness.

2. The church is a royal priesthood, a kingdom in which each subject serves as a priest.

3. The church is a holy nation, a people set apart to bear the name and nature of the holy God whom they worship and serve.

4. The church is God's own people, His cherished possession which ultimately will be redeemed to the praise of His glory (Eph. 1:14).

Something more than the institutional church meets the eye in these graphic terms. The church, for example, is *people* rather than a place or a building. It is a fellowship, not mere structures or organizations. The church means believers under the Master's mandate, touching the life of the world. Having conceded all that, a positive word needs to be said about the church local, the church on the corner, the people of God gathered for worship. This local fellowship provides the matrix for our nurture, instruction, fortification, and motivation for witness and work. Within the life of the local church we may find spots and wrinkles, but we find much more. We find loving people who touch our lives and push us gently toward God. We find admonition and counsel, which we need, stimulating fellowship and personal acceptance, without which life is impoverished. The church ministers to us in life's crises and it elevates our joys. Without doubt there is no other organization or association of persons so important for our growth as children of the Father.

The Royal Priesthood Has a Work to Perform in Christ's Name

There are priestly functions that arise out of the church's relation to Christ. John Calvin felt that we are "colleagues of His priesthood."[2] While some are authorized through ordination to proclaim the Word, the whole church is called to follow Christ and to share His ministry. Martin Luther believed our common anointing by the Holy Spirit makes us all priests.[3] Neither of these men meant that church members should all be amateur holy men and women. But they did declare that God's people are all "ministers." In doing so, they helped recover a basic New Testament truth that had been buried for centuries beneath a layer of dogma and clericalism. Fundamentally, there is one *laos* (people) of God and the duty and privilege of ministry rests upon this *laos*.

The Church Has a Reconciling Function to Perform

How could it be otherwise? The church itself is composed of persons who have been reconciled to God through the sacrificial deed of Christ. The cross, says Paul, has healed the rift between an estranged humanity and God. Reconciled to God, we are also reconciled to one another. This appears in the new humanity, the community of believers that transcends race, class, culture, and nationality. Christ is the bonding agent holding together persons of diverse backgrounds and varied temperaments (2 Cor. 5:14-20). This basic truth about the church, solidly rooted in Scripture, is not easy to implement.

Churches often feel comfortable when they follow a "consciousness of kind" policy. They reason that people are happier with their own kind. Sociologically, this separation of peoples may be understood. Theologically, it is a denial of the Spirit of Jesus and that love which embraces all persons.

The wife of a state governor once asked her pastor, "Do you know what prompted me to join this church?" "Please tell me," he replied. "Well," she said, "when we visited one Sunday morning, I was seated where I could see most of the congregation. I noted people simply dressed and I also saw people handsomely attired. I saw a large number of deaf persons, and across the way I noted several blind people. With all this mixture of persons, I suddenly had the notion that this is the kind of church Jesus would love! I wanted to be part of it."

Committed to a ministry of reconciliation and bearing the message of reconciling love (2 Cor. 5:18-19), the church is a fellowship rising above the things that fragment humanity. It is dedicated to the healing of old wounds. There is always a tension between the church and the world (humanity in its unregenerate state). But sharp tensions within the church or between churches is a denial of Christ. The priestly community, sharing the mediatorial function given by Christ, seeks to bring persons to God and to each other.

The Church Has Responsibility for Worship That Leads to Life Commitment

The church as a royal priesthood, is "to offer up spiritual sacrifices acceptable to God through Jesus Christ." In the biblical revelation, sacrificial terms are often used of worship. Worship, in turn, logically leads to a life that God approves. "He who offers a sacrifice of thanksgiving honors Me;/and to him who orders his way aright/I shall show the salvation of God" (Ps. 50:23). Worship includes offerings of money (Deut. 16:16-17), "the fruit of our lips" (Hos. 14:2), prayer and praise (Ps. 100:4; Col. 3:16), forgiveness and love (Mark 11:25; John 13:34-35), righteousness and mercy (Matt. 23:23). Spiritual sacrifices are in contrast to those material sacrifices which people often offer up to their gods. They indicate the devotion of the worshiper and are evidence of commitment to God.

Worship is at its best when the spiritual sacrifice presented to God is the individual himself. "I urge you, therefore, brethren, by the mercies of God, to present your bodies a living and holy sacrifice, acceptable to God, which is your spiritual service of worship" (Rom. 12:1). The term "spiritual service" comes from two Greek words (*logikēn latreian*) which mean a "worship rendered by the reason."[4] It is thus a rational choice, a deliberate act. A living sacrifice such as this pleases God.

Worship is perhaps the most important function of the church. Out of it emerges everything worthwhile that we do as a congregation. A fundamental part of worship is the interpretation and the hearing of God's revealed truth. Worship at its best brings us into the Divine Presence where hearts are cleansed and charged with fresh energy. Worship enables us to discern and accept our responsibilities. It fortifies and equips us for our ministry outside the sanctuary.

Worship that achieves the above goals can never be boring or dull. It is electric with the presence of God. Further, it becomes a suitable offering to God. Speaking of the sacrificial giving among the poor Macedonians, Paul noted their secret. "They first gave themselves to the Lord" (2 Cor. 8:5). People with that kind of spirit are in themselves acceptable sacrifices.

The Church Has Responsibility for a Faithful Witness to the Deeds of God

"You are . . . a royal priesthood, . . . that you may proclaim the excellencies of Him who has called you out of darkness into His marvelous light" (1 Pet. 2:9). The gospel had penetrated the Gentile world as Isaiah had predicted (Isa. 9:2). The "light of the knowledge of the glory of God in the face of [Jesus] Christ" (2 Cor. 4:6) had brought the Gentiles out of darkness. The mercy of God newly received had given them standing as the people of God (1 Pet. 2:10). Because of what God had done in them, they were given the mandate to evangelize.

Your witness and mine grows out of our personal experience. It is firsthand. "One thing I do know, that, whereas I was blind, now I see" (John 9:25). But our testimony points beyond that experience, as genuine as it is, to the matchless grace of God. It is Christ in us, using our verbal witness and our changed lives.

As a witnessing community, the church counts heavily upon individual members who take the gospel into homes, places of work, and society in general. Some pastors and churches effectively equip these members for their mission into the world. I saw a good example of this in a large Kentucky church where I was doing some supply preaching. The church had been without a pastor for months. But he and his staff had done an excellent work in equipping the people to minister and to witness. The church was fully alive. Its worship was dynamic. Its outreach was amazing. These people had become addicted to the work ethic as followers of Christ.

Responsibility for evangelism, the witness to God's grace, and the call to response rests squarely upon the shoulders of the church. Some of this witness is done through preaching. No man ordained for special ministry should minimize the place of proclamation in God's design for His church. The faithful souls who make up the congregation deserve the preacher's best homiletical effort. So do the people who drift into the church looking for hope and a clear word about God. Paul declared that his Gentile converts, won while he was "ministering as a priest the gospel of God" were an offering to God (Rom. 15:16). Any preacher would do well to make a similar offering.

The congregation's responsibility for evangelism is not limited to personal or pulpit proclamation. Through its worship, the people create a spiritual context within which unsaved persons are moved to believe on Christ. A spiritual dynamism created by the Spirit and marked by fervent prayer, praise, and clear speech mightily impresses the unbeliever. As a result, he feels convinced of the truth that is being proclaimed (1 Cor. 14:24-25). This is church-centered evangelism in its best form!

We are a royal priesthood, made so by Him who loved us and loosed us from our sins by His blood (Rev. 1:5-6). Because of Christ, our High Priest, we have received privileges and duties as priests. We are under His control and we are the instruments He uses to touch the life of the world. Some will be more effective instruments than others, but none are exempt from the mandate to be on mission in that world.

Surely there is hope for the church if we can recover the dynamic doctrine that has been the thrust of this message. Visualize the impact an army of priestly ministers can make upon the average community. It will take such an army to breach the wall of human problems found in the average community wherein the church ministers. Any Christian who has anything to give has abundant opportunity to give it daily. Nor do we work alone. Our life and work are linked with our great High Priest. We are His colleagues.

5

Multiplying
the Ministers

Exodus 18:13-26; Ephesians 4:11-12

"Let's open up the ministry!" So ran the title of a pastor's sermon. Jestingly, a church member commented, "I'm glad you are going to do that. I've always wanted to know what is on the inside of you fellows."

The pastor's sermon, however, was not describing a feat of surgery on a clerical body. Rather, he was dealing with a fundamental fact of the New Testament. The ministry and the mission of the church rest upon the shoulders of all God's people. The wide gap between clergy and laity has often weakened the church's work in the world. Furthermore, the division of the church into clergy and laity perpetuates the rift between sacred and secular. Under that arrangement, a few persons (clergy) handle holy things and the rest (laity) deal with the secular things of the world. That cleavage within the body of Christ belongs neither to the pattern of early Christianity nor to the intention of the church's Founder.

God never breaks up life into sacred and secular chunks. Nor does He intend that His work in the world should be done by a few selected persons. This is seen in a story out of Moses' life. Jethro, Moses' father-in-law, saw the younger man daily buried beneath a load of work as he handled disputes and problems among the Israelites. The old priest rebuked Moses for attempting the impossible. He strongly advised Moses to abandon his single-handed ministry for one involving a cadre of helpers. This biblical story has several implications for us.

A One-Man Ministry Has Limitations

The solitary leader such as a pastor, may be well-trained and highly gifted, but there are several factors that restrict him.

There Is a Time Limitation

The day has only so many working hours. Moses labored at full speed each day but never caught up with his duties. Pastors can be incredibly busy if they attempt all the work the church expects of them. Conscientious men of God compound the problem by setting impossible goals for themselves. The week is never long enough for them to accomplish all their planned work.

Richard Niebuhr, in a study of the church and its ministry, noted that ministers have become *pastoral directors*.[1] They have the full oversight of the church's work. Preaching is only one of their tasks. In large churches, the pastoral director may have paid staff members who share the work load. Even so, some pastors feel guilty if they do not fill their days with visitation, counseling, administrative duties, and sermon preparation. Pastors in smaller churches also carry heavy burdens, since they generally have no staff other than part-time clerical help. They must be all things to all people in the hope of pleasing some.

This was the situation in which Moses found himself. He "sat to judge the people, and the people stood about Moses from the morning until the evening" (Ex. 18:13). Few things are so frustrating as to end a busy day aware of the fact that many tasks are left undone. One person can do only what the time allows.

There Is an Energy Limitation

The weight of the day's labors often depletes the minister's strength. Problems unsolved or impossible of solution sometimes travel to bed with the pastor and rob him of rest. Thus he begins the next day with a deficit of energy.

Most people, however, draw small comfort from an overload. Jethro was appalled at Moses' daily routine. "What is this thing that you are doing for the people? Why do you alone sit as judge and all the people stand about you from morning till evening? . . . The thing that you are doing is not good" (vv. 14,17). According to the account in the Book of Numbers, Moses himself began to chafe under the burden of leadership. "Why have I not found favor in Thy sight, that Thou hast laid the burden of all this people on me? I alone am not able to carry all this people, because it is too burdensome for me" (11:11,14).

What pastor has not felt like that? Each day brings a pressure of concern for the church (2 Cor. 11:28) and the world. In addition, ministers encounter hostilities and cruelties (vv. 23-27) as they seek to correct society's ills and endeavor to make people over again. Their own strength is never enough to match the demands.

There Are Emotional Limitations

Daily, we experience a powerful drain upon the emotions. Our nervous energies are overtaxed. Even Jesus knew what it was to feel the exodus of energy (Mark 5:30).

Moses, at the end of each harried day of settling disputes, must have felt totally empty. This remarkable man was priest, army commander, medicine man, prophet, tribal chief, and judge. The people trusted him and needed him. Some cases that came before him were probably petty in nature: the violation of grazing rights, thefts of sheep or cattle, failure to pay debts, neglect of marriage payments and dowries, noisy children, and disturbances in the tents at night. A people recently enslaved were learning to work out adjustments to each other in a free society. And Moses sought daily to "judge between a man and his neighbor, and make known the statutes of God and His laws" (Ex. 18:16). A frightful responsibility rests upon such a person. It leaves one emotionally drained.

How does an overworked leader react when a critic tells him his act is "not good"? That kind of blunt criticism would flatten some persons. The human ego warms to praise and support, not censure and rebuke. The measure of the man Moses is seen in his willingness to be exposed, corrected, and guided by the older and more mature Jethro. Similarly, a pastor's degree of maturity is seen in his capacity to face his limitations, confess his inadequacy, and receive directions. His concern is for his people, not his own egotistical satisfaction.

A Multiple Ministry Ensures the People's Welfare

For one thing, it lightens the burden of the leader himself (Ex. 18:22). A host of fellow ministers brings a dimension of strength to the overburdened man of God. These colleagues are God's gift both to him and to the people (v. 23). The needs of persons are met with efficiency and dispatch by trained, experienced persons.

There are unique ministries that are performed by enlightened individuals who can empathize with persons being helped. A Christian couple lost an only child. They worked through their grief process and came away with their faith intact. Later, another couple, less secure in the Christian life, suffered a similar loss. Their pastor wisely called on the first couple for help in ministering to the distraught young parents. A single parent found the grace and peace of God as she faced the trauma of divorce and the realignment of her life. As a result, she became a ministering spirit to several other persons who themselves experienced the disruptions of divorce.

The average church generally has numbers of capable, gifted persons idling their motors. Moses was directed to look for assistants among the people, "able men who fear God, men of truth, those who hate dishonest gain" (v. 21). As is true in biblical analysis of leadership, the focus was on character and performance (see 1 Tim. 3). We do not know how long it took Moses to find this group of helpers. Was he surprised that they were so readily available? They had been present all the time, needing only to be called out.

The multiplication of ministers throughout the church never occurs automatically. Certain obstacles exist in the minds of people themselves. The world's image of religion and religious people, that these are not *macho,* creeps into the thinking of church members. Religion is good for women and children but not for big, strong men! Machiavelli felt that Christianity belonged to weaklings; Friedrich Nietszche called it a slave mentality. Some men who never heard of those two show a similar disdain for the Christian faith. They need to be reminded of the strong Christ and the heroic believers who have shown amazing strength of character and courage.

Another obstacle is the church's lack of vision and its failure to call men and women to adventuresome Christian living. There are more challenging Christian tasks than laying linoleum in the church kitchen, painting the church building, serving church suppers, and ushering each Sunday. The average community literally abounds with opportunities for healing, helping ministries. Human need is vast. Often, as one Detroit pastor put it, the shadow of the steeple falls across a human wasteland marked by misery, lostness, and despair. Our vision must be as broad as human need, and quick to draw on the church's resources for meeting it.

Church people are not always unwilling to fill ministry roles. Their reluctance may be due to a lack of training for these roles. Moses did more than select good, capable men to help him. He gave them directions for their tasks, made specific assignments, and turned them loose to work (Ex. 18:19-26). Like Moses, pastors are *equippers,* coaches who train their players and direct their skills. God's grand design for the church is that some should be "pastors and teachers, for the equipping of the saints for the work of service, to the building up of the body of Christ" (Eph. 4:11-12). Equipping (*katartismon*) means "to mend, fit out, complete, to make one what he ought to be." The equipper begins with what God has given. Through a process of training, encouraging, and developing the individual believer is fitted out for the work of ministry (*diakonia*).

Preaching may be the most emotionally satisfying task of the pastor. Equipping the people for the work of ministry, however, is his most crucial assignment. He may draw upon experienced teachers to assist in this developmental task, but the responsibility for getting it done rests on his shoulders. One reflective pastor who accepted such responsibility saw it as God's way of ensuring the spiritual welfare of his large congregation. Multiplying the ministers was a way of getting the church's work done.

Multiplying the Ministers Is True to God's Design for the Church

For centuries the church suffered because of the clergy's rigid control over sanctuary, sacrament, and Scripture. The Protestant Reformation, with its emphasis on faith, freedom, and the priesthood of all believers, took a giant step toward the recovery of the biblical pattern for the church. Within the twentieth century there has been a new focus upon the church as the whole people of God. The resurgence of lay religion, the innumerable lay groups, retreats, and institutes have made us aware of able men and women who desire a greater share in the institutional church's life.

Some pastors may feel threatened by the "upgrading of the laity." Capable men and women, it is true, may pose a threat to a pastor's program or person. Progressive movements may be blocked by reactionary laypersons. A pastor's problem is all the greater if he lacks patience or has exaggerated notions about his own position as God's man. A layman with such a pastor once remarked, "When it comes to a matter of God's will, my pastor seems always to have an inside track!"

The pastor's distinctive role is not usually in jeopardy if he is mature and doing his work in the spirit of Christ. Generally, he welcomes and facilitates the involvement of the people in varied ministries. Laypeople are "God's frozen assets." A wise pastor delights to have these assets thawed out and put to work. There are desirable results that benefit both pastor and church when this takes place.

For one thing, the layperson, caught up in the life of the world as the clergy are not, can interpret the world (its business and politics, goals and values, sins and hungers) to them.

Second, Christian persons form a driving wedge whereby the church and the gospel meet the world. As the church meeting the world, these persons function in strategic areas where decisions are made and the world's needful work is done daily.

Third, laypersons give both a verbal and a nonverbal witness to their faith. The quality and strength of their Christian lives make an impact upon people in the so-called secular society.

During Oliver Cromwell's reign in England the government's silver reserves were depleted. Needing silver for the production of coin money, Cromwell sent men across the land in search of it. They reported that the only silver available was in the statues of the saints in England's cathedrals. "Good," said Cromwell, "we'll melt down the saints and put them back into circulation!" Well, both the church and the world are best served when the saints are in circulation.

Jesus described His followers as salt and light. He knew, as we do, that salt and light are useful only as they are put in circulation. Stored up too long, salt may lose its distinctiveness. Kept under cover, a light serves no useful purpose (Matt. 5:13-16). Christ's followers are not called to lead isolated lives, aloof from the misery and lostness of the world (1 Cor. 5:10). They must keep close to those they would help.

The circulation of the saints requires that the church accept and implement God's design for His people. What do persons visualize when they hear the word *ministry?* Generally they think of men called of God and set apart by the church for pastoral or related service. The church selects a minister, pays him a salary, and expects him to perform certain functions. But ministry is more than prophets for hire. Ordination to ministry is an accepted and time-honored practice. But it neither defines nor limits ministry. In fact, some of the church's noblest ministers were never ordained. John Calvin, Charles H. Spurgeon, and Dwight L. Moody did quite well, though unordained. Nor to our knowledge was Jesus Himself ever ordained. Spurgeon went so far as to say that ordination is nothing more than laying empty hands upon empty heads!

The ministry of Christ and His church is *one,* though the ministers are legion. An excellent illustration of the one ministry with its varied representatives is found in Acts 18. Aquila and Priscilla, driven from Rome by edict of the emperor, came to Corinth. Because they were tentmakers, they invited Paul, a fellow tentmaker, to stay in their home. Without doubt, the apostle taught them what he knew of Christ and instructed them in matters of discipleship. After eighteen months, when he left for Ephesus, he took the couple with him. When Paul later departed from Ephesus, he left the work in the hands of Priscilla and Aquila.

The gifted Apollos came to Ephesus preaching and teaching the "things concerning Jesus, being acquainted only with the baptism of John. When Priscilla and Aquila heard him, they took him aside and explained the way of God more accurately" (Acts 18:25-26). Apollos the preacher was discipled by laypersons. Preachers can learn a great deal from ordinary laypeople! Luke's description of four ministering Christians indicates the spirit that should direct the church in cooperative ministry.

Churches need and benefit from pastors and trained staff members who bring to their positions a will to love and serve. They will likely perform no greater function than that of equipping the saints for the work of ministry. For the best church is that with a multitude of members who share Christ's mission and ministry according to their calling and gifts.

Horace Bushnell once said that the church needed one more great revival, a stewardship revival that would enlist millions. Well, we need another, even greater, a lay renewal that would gain millions of men and women for the diverse ministries needed in today's world. Then the people of God (*laos theou*) could literally turn the world upside down for Him.

6

A Church Worth Investigating

Acts 2:1-4; 3:1-10; 4:1-20

The church never escapes investigation. In a society filled with organizations, the church is viewed either as a popular institution or an unnecessary one. Friends of the church defend it. Critics question its freedom from taxation and government control. Neutral observers wonder about its contribution in the light of its claims. Scholars weigh the relative value of the church for "man come of age" and less dependent on God. Persons seeking a new church home carefully compare and investigate specific churches before planting their lives in one.

A young man, newly settled in a city, was looking for a church to his liking. After several Sundays of fruitless searching, he came to a church he had not visited. He came into the sanctuary as the people were reciting a prayer. "Lord," they intoned, "forgive us because we are sinners all. We have done that which we ought not to have done, and we have left undone that which we should have done. And there is no health in us." The young man relaxed with a sigh, "Thank God, at last I've found my crowd!"

With supreme insight, Jesus saw the inadequacy of His disciples for world conquest. They were indeed salt and light, but they were not yet ready to take on the world. Therefore, He counseled a period of prayerful waiting until the Spirit of God brought to them the power needed for their mission. For ten days they tarried in Jerusalem, studying the Scriptures (Acts 1:15-20), filling the gap left by Judas (1:21-26), and faithfully praying for God's promised blessing (1:14).

Then it happened as Jesus had promised. The wind of God blew, the fire fell, and the little group was radically transformed. They came alive with a Presence. People observed a drastic change in them. Small wonder some scholars feel that Pentecost was the day the church was born.

The Disciples Were Divested of Things Damaging to a Dynamic Ministry

At Pentecost the disciples were divested of things damaging to a dynamic ministry. There was a shaking up of their lives and an emptying of them, as one shakes a bucket of water and then pours it out.

Human weaknesses gave way to divine power. The entry of the Spirit marked the exodus of errors of judgment and faultiness of performance that impaired usefulness and influence. No claims of perfection could be made for the early disciples. But the Holy Spirit, the incredible power of God, altered their thinking, their behaving, and their performing. He does the same for all persons who are under His influence.

Prior to the Spirit's coming, blunders, notable imperfections, and striking uncertainties had characterized the disciples. On one occasion, they stood between Jesus and a group who were bringing children to Him. Their sharp rebuke of this group indicates the distance between their attitude and that of Jesus (Mark 10:13-14; Luke 18:15-17). At another time, when a band of Greeks came seeking Jesus, the cautious Philip took counsel of Andrew before he presented them to Jesus (John 12:20-22). Did he think non-Jews had no part in Jesus? William Barclay describes Philip as a man with "a warm heart and a pessimistic head."[1] John and James, men of violent temper, were well named "Sons of Thunder." Peter, despite his avowed loyalty to Jesus, was impulsive, quick-tempered, and capable of violence. Thomas possessed courage and a curious mind, but he lived with doubts and uncertainties.

None of Jesus' followers fully grasped the true nature of His mission. They were locked in to the Jewish concept of Messiah, right up to the ascension itself (Acts 1:6). Somehow they failed to understand the prophetic thrust of the Old Testament, Jesus' open declarations about His mission, or God's method of doing things. After His resurrection, Jesus walked with two disciples toward Emmaus. Was it their deep grief that cast a haze over their eyes so that they failed to recognize Jesus? Their words to Him are poignant: "We were hoping that it was He who was going to redeem Israel" (Luke 24:21). God had not conformed to their human expectations. Was it a similar disappointment that drove some of the disciples back to their fishing boats (John 21:2-3)?

Jesus showed remarkable patience with His fumbling slow-learning disciples. But even He was sometimes disturbed by their ineptness, weak faith, and failures. They belonged to that "unbelieving generation" that was unable or unwilling to lay hold of God's power. This is seen in the disciples' failure to heal the demon-possessed boy (Mark 9:14-29). Why they succeeded in other cases (Luke 10:17) and failed in this one is not clear. Jesus furnished a clue: Some situations yield only to prayer (Mark 9:29). Power is found in God, not in the person even of a devout believer.

We are never without human limitations and weaknesses. Amazingly, God uses us despite these. In aggravated forms, weaknesses may hurt our influence and damage the work of Christ. People are turned off by profane and empty speech, critical and austere attitudes, or bitter and unforgiving spirits. We easily excuse our ways: "I am only human"; "that's just human nature." But it is a nature not yet touched by Pentecost.

Bigotry and Narrow-Mindedness

The disciples, under the Spirit's impact, were divested of bigotry and narrow-mindedness. These twin evils obstruct the Kingdom by their harshness and exclusiveness. With considerable self-satisfaction, the apostle John once told Jesus, "Master, we saw someone casting out demons in Your name; and we tried to hinder him because he does not follow along with us" (Luke 9:49). As the apostle of love, John would later repudiate such a spirit. At the moment, he wanted no outsider cutting in on the distinctive ministry of Jesus and the twelve. Shortly thereafter, John and James, infuriated by the Samaritans who seemed hostile to Jesus, wanted to destroy their village by fire (Luke 9:51-55). The narrow-minded bigot is never so dangerous as when he acts religiously, believing that he is doing God's will.

Christianity may be as narrow as Christ and the way He proposes (Matt. 7:13-14). Closed minds are understandable if they have opened wide enough to close on Him. That sort of fixation on Christ broadens our minds to the whole truth of God. His Spirit in us opens our hearts to all those loved of God. The mind of Christ thus challenges bigotry and hatred of persons, narrow-minded sectarianism, and opposition to needed changes in society. An old settler once confessed, "There's been a heap of progress around here in the last thirty years, and I've been agin every bit of it!"

Jesus' followers looked for a kingdom political in character, material in nature, God's gift to Jews alone. Messiah, they believed, would come with a show of force and set up His kingdom in their midst. Are there not folks who still expect God to do the same thing? In a free society, individuals choose their own doctrinal positions. One person's preferences, however, should never mean denial of another person's freedom to differ. All of us are under the judgment of One who favors love of persons and breadth of spirit above rigid and exclusive orthodoxies.

Selfishness

Selfishness, a cardinal sin, beset Jesus' disciples. Each disciple wanted a slice of the coming kingdom. They often debated the question of who would be the greatest in the kingdom (see Matt. 18:1; Mark 9:33-34; Luke 9:46). Jesus challenged their view of greatness, a view akin to that held by the world. Self-centered persons scramble for positions near the top of the ladder. Weaker or less aggressive persons may be shoved aside or used by persons ambitious for power.

A driving ambition led John and James to move in ahead of their fellow disciples, seeking places of preeminence in the kingdom of God (Mark 10:35-37). "Grant that we may sit in Your glory, one on Your right, and one on Your left," they asked of Jesus. There was an audacity in that request. John and James showed little regard for their fellow disciples or for

Jesus, whose self-giving love was even then moving Him toward death.

Selfishness yields slowly! At the Last Supper and before the ascension, the disciples were still wondering about their places in the coming kingdom (Luke 22:24; Acts 1:6). Like us, an entrenched self-interest pushed them to the front, eager for every personal advantage.

Near the end of Jesus' ministry, *fear* caused the disciples to panic. To their credit, they had stayed with Jesus through some tense times when others had broken with Him because of fear, impatience, or disillusionment (John 6:60,66; 10:31-33,39; 11:16; 12:42-43). Yet each man in that little band lacked certainty about his relationship to the Master. During the Last Supper, when Jesus announced a betrayer in their midst, each man asked, "Lord, is it I?" (Matt. 26:21-22, KJV). At Jesus' arrest, according to the report, the disciples all "left Him and fled" (Mark 14:50; Matt. 26:56). Peter did make it to the courtyard of the high priest. But when confronted by Jesus' enemies, he vigorously denied any knowledge of the Master (Mark 14:54,66-72). The human instinct of self-preservation is a strong one. We rarely lose it.

Following Jesus' death, His followers went into hiding, going behind locked doors for fear of the Jews (John 20:19). From our secure position, it is easy to pass judgment on that little band of believers. When we look within our hearts, however, we find our own brand of fear, our caution about identifying with Him when the stakes are high. Public sentiment concerns us; outspokenness or direct action may bring sharp censure. So we betray our Lord not so much by loud denials as by cowardly silence. We, too, need a Pentecost to rid our lives of fear and timidity.

The Disciples Were Invested with Qualities
Needed for Their Mission

Biblical interpreters have long claimed that Jesus' resurrection is best attested by the wide-sweeping change that came over the church. The effective agent in that change was the Holy Spirit who came in fullness at Pentecost (see John 7:39).

Preoccupation with the form of the Spirit's manifestation must not direct attention away from the results of His work.

Power

The Holy Spirit brought a power to the waiting disciples. Wind and fire are two of the oldest symbols of God's presence (Ex. 19:16-18; 20:18-21; Ezek. 37:9-14). They symbolize the divine energy that flows through human lives, the power that both cleanses and moves us. Samuel Rutherford, an old English divine, remarked that "Seamen cannot create the wind, but they can hoist their sails to welcome it."[2] Sailboats move with the wind; Christians move under the power of the Spirit. The Jerusalem church's action cannot be explained apart from the Spirit of God, its driving force. That living Presence transforms the church from a group leading "tame lives and holding safe opinions" to a dynamic fellowship proclaiming a life-changing gospel.

Churches could get along without a lot of the things we hold essential. We could exist without air conditioning and cushioned pews. For centuries the church did. We might manage without salaried workers, ornate buildings, fleets of buses, or family life centers. Somehow the apostle Paul did. But we cannot justify our existence apart from the pulsating energy and the enlivening presence of God's Spirit. Look what He did for the little flock at Jerusalem. Unlettered, plain men—without degrees from recognized schools—took on the religious establishment, the crowd that murdered Jesus, the Gentile world, and even mighty Rome itself! "Not by might nor by power, but by My Spirit" (Zech. 4:6). That has to be the explanation for the incredible power that sustained Jesus' followers and flowed through their witness. For the endowment of power came not simply to produce ecstasy and gladness, but to enable the church to give witness concerning the living Christ (Acts 1:8). Latent powers for living and testifying are brought to the front by the Spirit. Schools of witnessing help us frame the message, but it is the Spirit who makes that message effective in people's lives (John 16:8-11).

"Lives of great men all remind us," so the poet Longfellow

said. Great Christian men and women enter and remain with their ministries because of the Spirit's sustaining power. Persons like Dwight L. Moody, Charles Spurgeon, Stanley Jones, Charles Finney, Lottie Moon, Billy Graham, and a host of others have revealed unusual spiritual power and fervor. The victorious life and witness of multitudes can best be explained in terms of the Holy Spirit in their lives. New energy, new vision, and effective witness always attend the Spirit's presence. It is that Presence which makes ordinary people into a church of the living God.

A Holy Boldness

The Spirit brought the disciples a holy boldness. They came out of that upper room to touch the life of the world. The most effective medication is worthless if it is kept bottled up! A monastic faith, kept within the walls of the sanctuary, fails to bless humanity. A Sunday morning brand of Christianity, so commonplace today, lacks the prophetic fire that will arouse the world's ire. It requires small courage to preach innocuous messages that skirt the real sins of the people or God's radical remedy for those sins.

Pentecost injected a quality of boldness into the preaching of Peter and John. They charged their hearers with responsibility for Jesus' death. Popularity seldom comes to persons who expose guilt and call for repentance. The audacity of the apostolic preachers is seen further in their refusal to abandon their proclamation. God has spoken, they declared, and civil and ecclesiastical authorities have no right to silence His messengers (Acts 4:1-20). The aura of public leadership failed to awe these men of God. Boldness and freedom in speaking the Word flow from the fullness of the Spirit (Acts 4:29-31).

Our world is full of problems that must be addressed by bold, intelligent Christian leaders. The ethical sins of our age need the kind of attention we give to theological sins! How can the church bring the mind of Christ to bear upon war and the arms race, disproportionate expenditures for weapons while world hunger persists, corruption and waste in business and government, or the build-up of greed and pride reflected in consumerism? What shall we say about crime and violence both in the media and in the streets? Shall we be silent about the waste in human life caused by alcohol and drugs? Must not the church deal redemptively with persons from broken families and with issues like child abuse and teenage delinquency? What about the loss of respect for standards of fidelity and chastity? These and other issues must be faced intelligently, honestly, and courageously. Biblical courage is telling it like it is—boldly witnessing to the saving gospel and the power of God to rescue persons from lostness, emptiness, and spiritual death.

Triumphant Faith

The Spirit of God brought the disciples a triumphant faith in the adequacy of Christ and His power to heal humanity's hurts. Peter and John, now on their own, bestowed healing upon a lame man "in the name of Jesus Christ the Nazarene" (Acts 3:1-10). This miracle was wrought on a man's physical body, but it was a sign of what could be done to a person spiritually. It also indicated that God's power, so fully revealed in Christ, now dwelt in His followers. Men of "little faith" (Matt. 6:30; 8:26; 14:31; 16:8) had come to be men of great faith.

Faith in the risen Lord gave Peter confidence to make a claim: "There is salvation in no one else; for there is no other name under heaven that has been given among men, by which we must be saved" (Acts 4:12). That truth is the basis for the church's mission and the individual's hope. Persons who believe in a deathless Christ are delivered from the fear of death. Persons committed to His unique authority as Savior and Lord wish to share that faith with all peoples everywhere.

Unity Within the Church

The Spirit of God created a unity within the church. "These all with one mind were continually devoting themselves to prayer, along with the women." . . . "When the day of Pentecost had come, they were all together in one place" (Acts 1:14; 2:1). Luke made a special point in referring to the presence of the women. In the new age of the church, both men and women received the Spirit, both sons and daughters were empowered to prophesy (Acts 2:17-18).

There is a unity created by the Spirit which we are to preserve in the bond of peace (Eph. 4:3), else we sin against Him. This oneness can be broken in two ways: (1) By conflict due to cliques, parties contending against each other, personality clashes, or sharp doctrinal differences; (2) by absenteeism, lethargy, and indifference. Where the church is divided by either of these, its spirit is dulled and its work is limited. In such case, it takes an act of God to set things right.

The Spirit creates genuine harmony within a fellowship. He brings a climate of love, forgiveness, acceptance, and thus togetherness. In a Spirit-controlled congregation, everybody is somebody. The enemy is Satan, not fellow Christians! And the world takes note of a church like that.

A Church Comes Under Investigation When Its Life Contrasts with That of the World About It

Strange new powers were at work in the congregation at Jerusalem. One man, a converted fisherman, preached a powerful sermon that led to 3,000 conversions. There were ventures in sharing economic goods, a grand generosity toward persons in need. Disciples performed works of healing. The excitement and congestion caused by the crowds disturbed the priests and Sadducees who had assignment from Rome to keep the peace. But imprisonment and threats failed to silence the Christian preachers or to stop the convocations. Can you imagine what effect the disciples' defiance of the Jewish council had upon the populace? Or upon the council? Furthermore, the church was reaching out to Samaritans and Gentiles. That irritated the Pharisees who advocated isolationism. Later, when Christians placed the Lord Jesus above lord Caesar, Rome itself brought the new movement under rigid scrutiny.

A church true to its Lord always gets attention. Sometimes this takes the form of hostility from the prevailing culture. In the second half of the twentieth century, the black church in America has led the way in Christian social action. America's social conscience has been aroused. Blacks and other ethnic groups have made some economic and legal gains. These gains have been resisted at times. Black churches and their leaders have experienced hostility and suffering. White churches that have entered the civil rights cause have also incurred opposition.

Churches that want to be noticed need only to live up to the gospel! They hardly need full-page ads in newspapers or billboard signs along the highway. The best advertisement for a church is its service record.

Investigations can be harsh and critical. They may also be positive, based on appreciation for the good work done for Christ. A church may catch the eye of the world simply because it is a humble, self-giving servant of the Spirit. Nonetheless, we must be prepared for those times when the people of God irritate a raw, godless society and provoke the wrath of persons. A church worth its salt is a church worth investigating.

7

The Wisest Person in Church

Proverbs 11:30; Daniel 12:2-3; John 1:35-42; 1 Peter 3:15-16

Second-hand book stores are a boon to booklovers. One man's purchases at such a store included a book entitled *The Soul Winner,* by Charles H. Spurgeon. He paid only a pittance for it, since it was marked and worn. A few days later he received a bill, evidently filled out by some meticulous clerk. The notation accompanying Spurgeon's work read: "One *Soul Winner—* Damaged—30 cents."

Many of us probably could be described like that. Preoccupied with secular duties or even religious activities, we give little thought or time to the church's primary task, that of witnessing to the saving grace of God. An ancient text of Scripture reads, "The fruit of the righteous is a tree of life,/And he who is wise wins souls" (Prov. 11:30). Translators and interpreters differ as to the proper reading of this text.[1] But the thought in the verse as quoted is most provocative. There is wisdom in winning persons over to God's side. This is a basic biblical fact, not dependent on any one Scripture. God has always been in the salvation business and He wants us to share His concern for a wayward humanity. Those who lead many to righteousness are bright lights in a dark world (Dan. 12:3). They are the wisest persons among us.

In all honesty, the New Testament uses the terms *witnessing* and *proclaiming* rather than soul-winning. Laypersons sometimes identify soul-winning as a work for trained, skilled persons who can bring individuals to a decision on the spot. They say in effect, effective soul-winners should gain trophies for Christ! Admittedly, some personal workers are more successful than others in introducing people to Christ and bringing them to salvation. Still, all Christ's followers are called to the witness stand. God's requirement is that we give faithful witness to Christ's death and resurrection, which is the heart of the redemptive message (Luke 24:45-48). We are interested in human responses to this message, but do not have to guarantee these.

The Supreme Heresy of the Contemporary Church Is the Silent Pew

"Let the redeemed of the Lord say so,/Whom He has redeemed from the hand of the adversary" (Ps. 107:2). Thus cried a grateful saint who was overwhelmed by the goodness of God. Why is there a button upon our tongues, closing down our witness to divine mercy? Is it because we have lost the sense of wonder over God's grace in saving us? Have we no concern for the falling spiritual birthrate within our churches?

Churches cannot be at ease in Zion when the God who wills our redemption also decrees that we witness concerning it. Ease is conducive to sleep and laziness. Caught up in this lethargy, churches become more like spiritual hospitals for convalescing members than an army of God on conquest for Him. Have you ever analyzed the prayer requests made during a Wednesday night meeting at church? As a rule they cover the sick or the crisis situations near and far, with an occasional reference to some event in the church's life. Seldom are there earnest requests that prayers be offered up on behalf of unsaved persons. The compassion for ill or troubled persons is certainly commendable. But why is there no travail among the saints, no agonizing intercession for persons outside the kingdom of God?

Perhaps this absence of intercessory prayer is related to the failure of Christians to witness. In 1984 it took thirty-nine members of one denomination to win one convert.[2] Imagine the plight of a cattle breeder if in a given year it took thirty-nine cows to produce one calf! Our problem is the silent church member who never gives a witness, never brings another person to Christ. Neglect is one way to destroy our witness and to bring slow death to the church. I once read about an artist who sought to put on canvas a portrait of church failure. He drew a baptistry covered by a large cobweb! When the baptistry remains dry, the church may be dying—from dry rot.

What is the pattern of the New Testament concerning the witnessing task? At the very outset of the Christian movement, two disciples of John believed John's witness and followed Christ. Immediately one of them found his brother and brought him to Christ (John 1:35-42). The experience of discovering new life through the Savior is too good to keep. It must be shared with others.

Andrew, like Jesus (John 4:5-42) engaged in one-to-one witnessing. Evangelism of this sort reaches people and feeds new life into the church. The New Testament pattern is clear from the Book of Acts. Everybody prayed; everybody bore witness to Christ; one man then stood up to preach and great things happened. The early church won its way in the pagan world not through organizations, institutions, wealth, or companies of trained, eloquent preachers. That church grew because hundreds of plain men and women spoke with genuine conviction everywhere and to anyone for Jesus Christ.[3]

Gifted preachers are an asset to the church, and mass evangelism (especially in the electronic age) is a viable method of reaching people. But neither is a replacement for the vocal and life-style witness of the individual Christian. The church must, in recognition of this fact, encourage persons to engage in witnessing, and help them develop skills for it. This is one way to halt the falling birthrate in the church and to correct the heresy of the silent pew.

The Wisest Man in Church Is Sustained by Certain Basic Convictions

These convictions are a part of his Christian life, threads that make up the fabric of his being.

Witnessing Is Every Christian's Job

Each of us is a potential voice for Christ. He has rescued us from sin, brought us into the righteousness of God, and set us apart for good works (Eph. 2:1-10). We can tell others what has happened in our experience, what we now know firsthand about God's power to lift us out of futile, empty living. That is a witness's assignment. You can never drive people into giving that witness, nor can you shame them enough to break their silence. The will to testify to saving grace comes from within. Generally, we talk freely about things we believe and value, things that grip us and motivate us. This is true not only of our initial grace experience, but of the adequacy of Christ for the pressures and demands of each day. Witnessing brings people up to date on the Lord's active presence in our daily life.

Luke ascribes the expansion of the early church to the willingness of people to talk about Jesus. Believers were scattered in all directions due to persecution, and wherever they went they gave their witness. These persons were plain, common folks, not the original apostles. Later, Paul mentioned the strategy of teaching "publicly and from house to house, solemnly testifying to both Jews and Greeks of repentance toward God and faith in our Lord Jesus Christ" (Acts 20:20-21). In our urban society this kind of witness becomes difficult. People fear to open their doors to strangers. Apartment and multiple housing units employ security measures to keep visitors at bay. In addition, a philosophy of pleasure and a desire for anonymity freeze out the Christian witness.

In the face of obstacles, Christians must be inventive and find ways to penetrate the barriers that people erect. These techniques must be sensible and marked by courtesy. But the will to witness leads one to find a way.

People Everywhere Need the Good News About Christ

Offensive as it sounds, life without Him is lost. The root of evil in society is the unregenerate heart. The life hurtling toward eternity is in danger and its course must be altered. We gain nothing in our attempts to change people unless we recognize that they are sinners, alienated from God, captive to Satan, helpless to save themselves.

Every generation, it seems, has to learn for itself that there are no substitutes for that new life created by the Holy Spirit. We keep hoping for a changed society through education, redistribution of wealth, cultural diffusion, or the alteration of life through drugs and technology. These all avail little so long as the inner life goes unchanged. Jesus' words ring clear across the ages: "You must be born anew." He Himself spoke of life apart from God as lost, perishing, and under judgment. The opposite of this desolation is moral renewal, hope, peace, security, and positive living.

With a lively memory of past guilt and lostness, we Christians should be able to talk about the transformation Christ has brought to us. Gratitude alone should cause us to give what Peter terms a "defense" for our faith (1 Pet. 3:15). "Defense" or *apologia* suggests the practice of early believers who gave an *apology* for the Christian religion. Apology in this case simply meant a reasoned, convincing, factual account of the faith one held. Two dimensions of that "defense" stand out: the truth as it is in Jesus Christ (objective fact), and one's own personal experience of forgiveness (subjective fact). Such an apology would now serve us well, confronted as we are with a pluralistic society that includes many ethnic groups from non-Christian lands.

Every neighborhood has its evangelistic opportunities. Once I visited a church member whose business life absorbed most of his time and energies. Our conversation centered upon one of his neighbors, a family divided in its religious affiliations. Said he, "I rather think the husband is not a Christian at all. I should know, shouldn't I?" Then he thoughtfully remarked, "I must admit that I have lots of opportunities in this block. There are several unsaved, unchurched people near my own house!" In our "live and let live" society, we may not be so aware of our own neighbor's spiritual alignments. Most likely, however, we know one or many who make no claim to being Christian. Dare we try to penetrate the curtain of casualness behind which they hide?

The Christian Witness Realizes the Urgency of Personal Decision Regarding Jesus Christ

That decision is fraught with destiny. Jesus opened His ministry on a sobering note: "The kingdom of God is at hand;

repent and believe in the gospel" (Mark 1:15). Later, He put the truth even more emphatically. "Unless you repent, you will all likewise perish" (Luke 13:3,5). Three of Jesus' memorable parables detailing the divine love for persons indicate that without this love, individuals are *lost*. The plight of unredeemed persons must disturb our souls. The destiny of such persons, if they fail to turn from their present course, is hell itself. Even the most loving, person-oriented Christian must face this fact, for it comes to us on the authority of Christ and is woven into Scripture.

Modern distaste for the doctrine of hell stems in part from pictures of hell as God's torture chamber for damned souls. This view of hell owes more to medieval theology than it does to Scripture or the nature of a loving Father. In our Western world, heaven and hell get more attention in profane and jesting speech than they do from the pulpit! Furthermore, the focus in our culture on science and technology rather than on theology has lessened our preoccupation with life beyond. There is a confidence in man's ability to manage his life with little need for God and less apprehension about the future.

We cannot, however, dismiss biblical teaching because it has been misinterpreted, ignored, or proved offensive to our tastes. Sincere students of the Scriptures marshall the evidence and seek to understand it. What does the graphic, symbolic language of the Bible mean in regard to hell? Those symbols represent something real, perhaps more awesome than any literal interpretation itself.

In its essence, hell is final separation from God. It is separation from the fellowship of the redeemed by a fixed gulf (Luke 16:26). Hell is loneliness, regret, and remorse without the possibility of repentance. What we are talking about begins in this life, and some of us know it firsthand!

Hell holds no terror for souls that are secure in God's love. And the Christian witness, though believing in hell, knows that more persons are won by love than by threats and fear. Still there is a legitimate appeal to fear. A parent is wise to instill fear in a child whose careless conduct can bring injury or death to the little one. Sensible persons sound the alarm when a house is burning down around its occupants. Knowing the fact of judgment and the fear of the Lord led Paul to *persuade* men (2 Cor. 5:10-11).

There is a stubborn perversity about human nature that calls for strong warnings against the rejection of divine love. Human beings, of all earthly creatures, are free to obey or disobey God. The winds and the waves obey His voice; the earth and the heavens follow His will; the seasons come and go at His bidding. But human beings for all their finiteness, can repudiate God and turn away that love which saves. They are free to do that. They are not free to escape the consequences of the choices they make.

The knowledge of all this surely motivates us to give witness to Him who alone can take hell out of life and replace it with heaven.

The Christian Witness Is Convinced that Christ Alone Can Save Human Life

No man-made scheme can rescue persons from their evil. No self-help program can cleanse life or lift it above an "activated depravity." Jeremiah put it plainly: "A man's way is not in himself;/Nor is it in a man who walks to direct his steps" (10:23). Neither our personal efforts nor our religious performances are enough to remove the demon from our hearts.

While on a witnessing assignment, a friend and I called on a couple in an apartment house. The young people belonged to another church group but had been visiting the downtown Baptist church. Because they were unfamiliar with our evangelical terminology, we were discussing the meaning of salvation and the nature of human response. One of the listeners remarked, "You keep talking about 'being saved.' What do you mean by that?" Wishing to begin with what I felt was a commonplace verse, I asked, "Do you know John 3:16?" "No, I do not," she honestly replied. So we began at that point. An incident like that startles one. How many people are there, in how many churches, who do not know the basics about Jesus Christ and personal salvation? Small wonder that Elton Trueblood once declared that the church itself is a fertile field for missions!

Christian witnesses go out bearing a name, confident of the saving power of Christ. "There is salvation in no one else; for there is no other name under heaven that has been given among men, by which we must be saved" (Acts 4:12). There are many great names associated with religion: Moses, Muhammad, Buddha, and lesser lights like John Smith and Mary Baker Eddy. But there is no name like that of Jesus who rescues persons from the depths of sin and grants them the gift of eternal life. This conviction, rooted in our own experience, motivates us to witness with faith and fearlessness.

The Wisest Person in Church Engages in the Most Rewarding Work in the World

Personal Witnessing (Winning Persons to Christ) Revitalizes the Christian Life

Our faith grows as we give it away. The experience of sharing the gospel deepens our conviction of its adequacy.

Someone may resist, saying, "But I am only a plain, untalented person." Then you are the sort of person God often uses. Ordinary individuals sometimes introduce to Christ men and women who become giants in the kingdom. Simon Peter outshone Andrew, yet it was Andrew who brought Peter to Jesus. Back of the great Augustine was his mother, Monica. An aged monk helped Luther find God's forgiveness and Luther became a key figure in the Protestant Reformation. The world-renowned Dwight L. Moody was brought to Christ by a Sunday School teacher. Who knows but that some convert of yours may become a powerful leader in the kingdom? Even if that never happens, your faithfulness in sharing the good news will gain some for Christ. And it will serve to keep your Christian life fresh and growing.

Winning Persons to Christ Helps Create a More Righteous Society

We will never have a better world until we have better people. Critics may scorn the idea that human nature can be changed. That is mere idealism, they charge. But efforts to change human society and world conditions without changing human nature are destined for failure. Any hope of restructuring society depends upon changing the individual, and that calls for an act of God.

When Jesus reached Zacchaeus, that dishonest little tax-collector was radically changed. We are told that he immediately inaugurated some new economic practices in his life, and most likely in his business as well. We may assume that his conversion affected his household also.

John W. Suttle, my father in the ministry, told about his strategy in winning a rather notorious sinner. The man was given to heavy drinking, gambling, and other iniquitous practices. But he had a godly mother who joined with the pastor in efforts to reach her son. Pastor Suttle learned that the man loved to fish, so much so that he consented to go fishing with a Baptist preacher! The two men went on several fishing trips together. One day as they were jack fishing, the big fellow laid down his rod and reel and asked the little preacher, "Are you fishing for jack or for me?" "I'm fishing for you," replied Mr. Suttle. They pulled the boat over to the bank and there the pastor led him to faith in Christ. When a disciple of Satan like that becomes a follower of Christ, it sets off ripples of change in a home, a business, and a community. That is Christ's way of plundering the house of Satan (Mark 3:27), and building up His own kingdom.

The Christian Witness Deals with Eternal Issues

There is no end to the good done in reaching persons for Christ. Even when we fail to win our hearers, we have planted imperishable truth in their minds. Like healthy seeds placed in soil, that truth may yet germinate and produce results.

There can be no greater reward than the personal satisfaction and divine commendation that follow a faithful Christian witness. To invest in human lives, to help persons find the freedom and joy of eternal life—there is no parallel to this. A person's deeds are somewhat like monuments. People remember us for the things we do. But so many of these monuments are perishable. Buildings made of wood or stone suggest an

architect's fame but one day they will crumble. Lovely paint-
ings attest an artist's skills but they eventually fade or face
destruction. Economic empires are a tribute to great financial
wizards, but both the empire and the emperor are soon forgotten.

There is something eternal about the work of men and
women who win persons to Christ. The mother of George W.
Truett, one of yesterday's greatest preachers, was a simple
woman, quiet, and unassuming. But one Sunday when her
church gave recognition to its personal workers, more than
twenty individuals came to stand by her side. Through her
efforts she had won each of them to Christ. A small investment
of time produced a wealth of eternal goodness.

The name of Michelangelo stands for greatness in religious
art. As a lad, Michelangelo assisted in the preparations for a
dinner attended by artists and sculptors. He took the butter
and carved it in the form of a crouching lion. Impressed by the
artistic design, the men wanted to know who had created it.
The trembling youth was brought in and applauded. One of the
professionals said to him, "Young man, don't waste your time
on perishable butter. Work on imperishable marble." Michelangelo took that advice and the world continues to sing his
praises.

The wisest person in church is the one who regularly works
to win individuals for Christ. The most fortunate person is the
one who has a friend concerned for his eternal welfare. Those
persons who let down the gospel net as fishers of men know the
deepest joy and merit the fullest commendation of their
Master.

8

Saints
in Strange Places

Philippians 4:22

Few people would go looking for saints in the luxurious licentious palace of an emperor! For that reason, Paul's closing words in the Philippian letter grab our attention. "All the saints greet you, especially those of Caesar's household." Saints belong in churches, on pedestals or stained-glass windows, but never in Caesar's household. One might as well look for saints at a raucous political convention, a bartender's association, or an adult movie house.

Who were those saints of whom Paul wrote? They were persons serving in some capacity within Caesar's household. According to J. B. Lightfoot, "Caesar's household" was a term for people in Roman government from the highest ranking officials to the lowest slaves. Some of the saints, for example, might have been members of the guard.[1] Possibly Paul was writing from a prison near the palace, having been moved from his private lodging (Acts 28:30). Christians serving in the imperial household would, therefore, have opportunity for fellowship with the apostle. Some of them likely were friends who saw him frequently.

Evidently, the "saints" were part of the church of Rome, a church which neither Paul nor Peter founded. "It is the growing consensus of scholarship, both Protestant and Roman Catholic, that Hellenistic Jewish converts from Palestine and Syria brought the gospel to Rome at an early date, possibly by A.D. 30."[2] Thus, when Paul arrived in that city, he found a church and friends who undergirded him.

The presence of a little band of saints in Caesar's household impresses a number of significant facts upon our minds.

Adversity Is No Deterrent to the Gospel

Planting the Christian faith in the heart of the Roman Empire was a bit like anchoring the battle flag at the enemy's command post. Christ's true followers are not weaklings. They are described as people who can tough it out. In 2 Timothy 2:3-6 they are likened to soldiers, athletes, and rugged farmers. There is nothing anemic about persons in those professions.

Think of the courage required to confess faith in the Lord Jesus when loyalty was demanded by lord Caesar! It puts us to shame because of our tepid Christianity, our easy church membership in a land where religion is popular, or our refusal to hear or take seriously the commands of Christ.

Paul could appreciate those believers in Rome. He knew what adversity can do to hinder the gospel's advance (Rom. 15:22; 1 Thess. 2:18; 2 Tim. 4:14-16), and how much is required of persons who acknowledge their commitment to Christ in the face of hostility. But adversity failed to silence Paul's tongue. There is no record of Paul complaining to God about his hardships. Writing to the Philippian Christians from prison, he talked about peace, joy, forbearance, and contentment (Phil. 4:4-12). That is hardly the counsel of a person broken by adversity or angry with God. The secret of his fortitude is found in these words: "I can do all things through Him who strengthens me" (v. 13).

Small wonder that Paul and the saints in Caesar's household got along so well. They knew what it was to live dangerously. Adversity failed to break their spirit or deflect them from loyalty to their Master. Surely there were times when they felt fear or even discouragement. The best of God's children have moments like that. John the Baptist did. He had proclaimed Jesus as God's anointed, and yet in Herod's dungeon he had doubts and misgivings about the Messiah. Elijah the iron prophet, running from wicked Jezebel who had threatened his life, crumpled under a juniper bush and prayed to die. Momentary fears and doubts, however, do not destroy great souls.

Indeed adversity makes the person stronger and sturdier, like the wind that toughens the oak. God never produces saints in hothouses, carefully sheltered from heat or storm. It is in the crucible that the gold is refined and the dross consumed. Some persons cannot be understood apart from the role that adverse circumstances have played in shaping their lives.

Wayne Oates, creative scholar and pioneer in pastoral care, illustrates this point. In his book, *Struggle to Be Free,* he traces the events, many of them hostile and bitter, that made up his crucible. Born into a culture of poverty, growing up without the guidance of a father, cutting his way through an unfriendly environment, Oates developed an independence of spirit mingled with compassion for persons. Coping with a tough world, he developed that free, indomitable spirit that has carried him to unusual success as minister, teacher, and writer.

Adversity equips us to help persons who themselves stumble upon hard and trying times. This is one thing the fellowship of the saints can do for us. Did that little *ekklēsia* (church or *called-out ones*) in Rome seek out Paul to befriend him and bolster his spirit? Or, caught up amid the pressures of Caesar's household, did they seek comfort and guidance from an elderly Christian who had lived for years with persecution and tension? Most likely, the contacts were mutually beneficial.

One of the most respected and honored basketball coaches of this decade is John Thompson of Georgetown University. This man is black, coaching an exclusively black team at a predominantly white school. Coach Thompson has a dual concern for his players: excellence in athletics and proficiency in academics. He is dedicated to the preparation of young men for functioning in society, not just on a basketball court. Back of this coach's penchant for excellence is his own growing-up experience. As a child he was such a poor student that an educator told his mother, "This boy isn't educable." Reacting to that cruel indictment and the cultural deprivation within his own home, John Thompson began the long struggle that brought him two college degrees and, ultimately, his present position. Adversity never broke his spirit. Rather, it led him to that excellence which he now demands of his players. Because some of them have come from backgrounds similar to Thompson's, he is all the more a model for them.[3]

Not only does adversity equip persons for ministry, it provides opportunity for witnessing to Christ. Persons who handle their difficulties and sufferings with courage make a profound impact on our lives. Death was lurking in Paul's cell, waiting only for the emperor's word. But no fear of death could keep the apostle from witnessing to the soldiers, slaves, and other persons about him. Thomas Carlyle spoke words that apply to Paul. Said he of a person who speaks of spiritual things, "It is among the beautifulest, most touching objects one sees on the Earth." This disposition to introduce persons to Christ, so Dwight L. Moody thought, is certain evidence of an individual's salvation. If this witness emerges from the context of adversity, it may the more readily gain the attention of the listener.

Adequacy of the Gospel

Saints in Caesar's household clearly attest the adequacy of the gospel. If the power of Christ can reach persons in the emperor's palace, there is hope for all of us. God is forever pulling persons out of slums, the homes of peasants and laborers, cotton mill settlements, and tenant farm families, as well as king's palaces and rich people's dwellings. No places are off limits to the Spirit, and no individuals are shut off from divine mercy. God can take the ordinary stuff of human life and make saints of it. He did it at Rome; He does it today.

Let us make clear the fact that saints are not out of this world. They are plain people who are mightily involved in changing this world. The New Testament view of sainthood sets the record straight, and in doing so challenges some of the ecclesiastical definitions of saintliness. One of those definitions observes that a saint is "one who is in enjoyment of the beatific vision and has been presented by the church for the public worship of the faithful." There are no such persons in the New Testament! Saints are not people with halos. Nor are they perfect persons, sitting in self-righteous judgment of others. Reinhold Niebuhr once remarked that a saint is the wife of a man who thinks he is one!

Real saints possess a natural goodness and graciousness. They are not austere, dull, straitlaced and pretentious souls.

Generally, they make no claims to goodness and often are unaware of it in themselves (Matt. 25:37-39). They are drawn from the rank and file of humanity. Saint Matthew, we know, was a tax-collector; Saint Mark, merely "a young man"; Saint Luke, a Greek physician; Saint John, a hot-tempered person nicknamed "Son of Thunder." In their own generation they were just ordinary people, hardly candidates for the sort of sainthood given them later.

Why, after all, does the New Testament call Jesus' followers *saints?* It is one of the most common designations used of them. The term *hagios* applies to a person worthy of veneration or reverence. That veneration is not self-generated. Rather, a saint is one who has a connection with God. God alone makes one "holy." Further, saintliness is maintained by association with God. God has exclusive rights to the life of the saints. They are set apart for His service.

In a collective sense, the term *hagioi* (saints) once applied to Israel. It is now used of Christians who partake of the divine salvation, share God's purpose, and bear His name among the nations. Seen from a moral perspective, saints are called to be "pure, sinless, upright, and holy" (see 1 Pet. 1:16; 1 Cor. 1:2). That is a high ideal, and the New Testament records show how difficult it was to attain. There was, for example, contention and strife in the Corinthian congregation. Simon Peter dealt with the lies and hypocrisy of Ananias and Sapphira. Paul grieved over the worldliness of Demas and the defection of John Mark. John had problems with the arrogant, dictatorial Diotrephes. Even the foremost disciples had moments when they dropped below the standards set for saints. After all, saints are not cut from perfect cloth; they are cast from common clay.

Saints are plain people made over again by divine grace. They share the simplicity of their Master who went about doing good and healing those oppressed by the devil (Acts 10:38). How quickly we forget the origins of the humble Galilean carpenter, and His identity with Palestine's toiling masses! Jesus came from the peasant class and appealed to the common people. They heard Him with gladness and hope. Now see what we have done with Him. We have hidden Him within elaborate rituals, obscured Him by ornate clerical garb and costly temples, and buried Him beneath dogmas and creeds. Where is the carpenter clad in working garments, the plain-speaking teacher people loved to hear, the bighearted man whose compassion allowed Him to overlook none?

The saints are people like this Christ, and they come from all levels of life. In His day Jesus seemed to have had a fondness for lowly company, persons whom the religious establishment had written off. He made saints out of tax-collectors, lepers, mentally deranged persons, prostitutes, and profane fishermen. He also took a brilliant but fanatical Pharisee and turned his life around completely. That man, Saul of Tarsus, believed mightily in the gospel which had transformed him. But he never ceased to marvel at Christ's power to change human nature. "Do you not know," he wrote the Corinthian believers, "that the unrighteous shall not inherit the kingdom of God? Do not be deceived; neither fornicators, nor idolaters, nor adulterers, nor effeminate, nor homosexuals, nor thieves, nor the covetous, nor drunkards, nor revilers, nor swindlers, shall inherit the kingdom of God. And such were some of you; but you were washed, but you were sanctified, but you were justified in the name of the Lord Jesus Christ, and in the Spirit of our God" (1 Cor. 6:9-11).

Paul's description of Corinthian life (vv. 9-10) indicates the deepest sort of degradation. Yet the grace of God reached some of those Greeks and worked miracles in their lives. The thoroughness of the divine operation is shown by the terms *washed, sanctified, justified.* Their baptism attested their spiritual cleansing and the fact that they had been made right with God. Because of amazing grace, these Corinthians could now be called "saints" (1 Cor. 1:2).

The Saints Travel the Victory Road

That sounds unbelievable. How could that small group of Christians in Caesar's palace or the little pocket of believers in Graeco-Roman cities be viewed as victors in anything? Conquering people generally have strong, masterful leaders. Could that be why Rome initially disregarded Christianity as a threat to the empire? Jesus before Pilate and Jesus on His cross seemed helpless enough. Paul the tentmaker, bothered by some bodily deformity and never impressive as a speaker (2 Cor. 10:10), might be a nuisance but not a major problem for Caesar. Mighty Rome dispatched any real troublemakers. There were crosses, lions, swords, or other means of wiping out resistance.

How then can we speak of Christians as victors?

1. They are linked with the power that creates and controls all things. They are sons and daughters of a Heavenly Father and have access to Him at all times. Caesar has his royal family and his court. Christians are a royal priesthood, "a kingdom and priests" to God (see 1 Pet. 2:9; Rev. 1:6). Every believer is a priest and a king! That is what the biblical writers are saying. Even the pauper is a king, possessing the only true riches. The lowliest layperson is a priest, made so by "Him who loves us, and released us from our sins by His blood" (Rev. 1:5).

Some subways use big signs that direct passengers to follow the red line leading to the trains. Even so, the saints come into eternal life by traveling along a crimson road. This is the red road of sacrifice first traversed by Christ. But the path we tread may call for some sacrifice of our own, similar to His though never so great. The world's noblest sacrifice led to the most signal victory. Whether in Caesar's household or in our own hometown, we seldom sing the song of victory without also singing the song of the Lamb (sacrifice).

2. Our victory consists of an imperishable heritage. The world may deprive us of fortune, home, job, friends, or even reputation. But nothing can "separate us from the love of God, which is in Christ Jesus our Lord" (Rom. 8:35-39, KJV). God does not lose or cast aside His trophies. Through His great mercy, He has granted us "an inheritance which is imperishable and undefiled and will not fade away" (1 Pet. 1:4). That fact undergirds our hope and puts iron in our blood. We are kept by the power of God—nothing can destroy us.

It is this kind of faith that keeps us strong whether in Caesar's household, or in any other difficult circumstance. We believe that God has a grip on our souls. That steadies us, even when our world is shaky or about to break up around us.

Did you ever walk a swinging footbridge above a torrent of water? My first experience of that came near Frankfort, Kentucky. I was a student at The Southern Baptist Theological Seminary in Louisville and served a small rural church on weekends. Some kind church member would provide me a prophet's chamber each Saturday night. The road to many farm homes crossed a creek. In the absence of a bridge, the creek was easy to ford except in rainy seasons. Then the driver would park the car, cross on an elevated footbridge, and walk to the farm home. Once I found myself on such a footbridge, carrying a heavy suitcase. The combination of high, rushing water and the swinging of the bridge shook me up. I felt near panic! I realized I could make it only by setting the suitcase down and pushing it with my feet, while I held to the sides of the bridge. What helped even more was looking up and across at the destination I hoped to reach. When I fixed my eyes on that target, I found help in completing my journey.

Life needs its fixed points and certainties. Without these, the saints know no steadfastness and lack confidence in their walk. Do you wonder why the early Christians were so bold in the face of hostile circumstances? Well, they knew where they had come from—the kind of persons they once were. They also knew where they were going. It is hard to terrify people who are unafraid of hardship and death. Those believers felt that Jesus had won the ultimate victory, the conquest of death itself. They could look the worst enemies in the face and know they had been conquered by Another. Nothing, not even death itself, could break their tie to the Master.

Girolamo Savonarola, fifteenth-century Italian reformer and preacher, was charged with heresy and condemned to die. His accuser, the bishop of Vasona, bungled the customary formula, "I deprive you of the church militant." He added the words, "And the church triumphant." The martyr rightly replied, "Of the church militant, yes; but of the church which is triumphant, no; that does not belong to you."[4] It belongs to God, and He grants His children the right to share in its victory.

The last enemy to be destroyed, so Paul wrote, is death. But it will be destroyed! Indeed, its power over life has already been checked by Him who died and rose again. "Because I live, you shall live also" (John 14:19), He promised. Biblical faith never denies the reality of death but it hurls this taunt, "Death, you yourself shall die." For the saints, the door of death proves only an entry to the Father's house.

3. God's people at their best make an impact on society. Caesar might have sneered at the little band of Christians, but, in time, Christianity undermined and destroyed the old order. The strategy used is still a viable one: Drain off a few million souls by the attraction of a new and higher allegiance. We know the story. Under the Emperor Constantine, in AD 312, Christianity was made the state religion. That, however, might never have happened but for one fact: A small group of Christians lived like saints in Caesar's household, long before a Caesar became friendly to their faith.

The Face of Christ in Human Need

Matthew 25:31-46

The family album keeps alive the memories of persons long since departed. We trace the development of our children by photographs taken at various stages of their growth. In the absence of photos, we construct the image of persons as they are described by others. Individuals become real through such visualization.

Nowhere in Scripture do we have a description of Jesus. No New Testament writer mentions his height, the color of His eyes and hair, or the quality of His voice. There is a strange silence about His physical form, facial features, or the kind of clothes He wore. The focus is upon His words and deeds, as though God wanted us to know the essential person rather than the external trappings.

What made Jesus become real to you? Jesus is often trapped in our religious systems and encased in our creeds and liturgies, but not always known to us personally. Then one day all the superficial covering is torn away and He stands forth in our midst in all His glory. He was there all the time; we just failed to see Him.

An ancient fable illustrates the point I am making. A dying father left his son a huge wooden idol. The young man faithfully worshiped this idol, hoping for some tangible rewards. But he received none of the wealth he expected. One day, in an impatient rage, he knocked the idol from its lofty pedestal. The idol was broken in the fall and a fortune in gold coins were scattered about the man's feet. The wealth had been there all the time, hidden from his view.

Ironically, religion and religious systems sometimes hide

Christ from us. We venerate dogmatic views of God, the Bible, and the church—the things that are important for belief and behavior. A flurry of religious acts replace obedience grounded in the sense of God's living presence (Matt. 7:21-23). But Jesus has a way of shattering our notions about God and religious duty. In the parable of the last judgment, He put a finger upon the kind of living God views as important. Since this is a parable, we must guard against an excessive literalism in the interpretation of its details. The main message, however, seems fairly obvious.

Jesus Christ Comes to Us in the Form of Human Need

And He comes *now*. That is the unmistakable thrust of the parable.

Admittedly, the parable has a future reference. The King will come in all His glory. Every eye shall see Him. History's last word, the Bible insists, will be spoken by God. The vaunted boasts of human beings will be shattered. God's purposes ultimately will be realized. Human intentions will survive only as they are in line with God's. All creation will recognize the Creator and every knee will bow to Him (Phil. 2:10). The details of that final judgment are known only to God. The Bible's references to the end of the age and the coming of the kingly Judge are couched in figurative language. Human speculations lack reliability and bleed off energies that should be given to more authentic pursuits. We simply cannot lock Jesus within a system or restrict God to our theological patterns. If God will not be limited even to the life of Jesus (John 14:28) or the Scriptures, He will hardly be bound to any system we devise.

The coming of the kingly Judge in all His glory is a future reality—that is true. But judgment is also a *present work of God*. The process goes on constantly. We are being evaluated in terms of our deeds. Do Jesus' words limit this judgment to His followers? Is it a judgment upon the Jews, or does the term *nations* here apply to the Gentiles as it frequently does in Scripture? Most likely "all the nations" means *all* the nations!

There is one standard of judgment disclosed in this parable: love reflected in a gracious ministry to persons. This standard applies to individuals, churches, nations, and the whole world. "All the nations will be gathered before Him" (Matt. 25:32). It is difficult to argue with the inclusiveness of those words. And as persons engage in sincere, loving acts in behalf of others, they come into a consciousness of Christ. That is one specific way He becomes known to us. The "glory of God in the face of Christ" (2 Cor. 4:6) shines forth clearly as we minister helpfully to needy persons. "To the extent that you did it to one of these brothers of Mine, even the least of them, you did it to Me" (Matt. 25:40).

Observe that Jesus' reference is to deeds, not creeds, to acts rather than words. Sound doctrine is imperative; verbalization of our faith is important. But "others will not care how much we know until they know how much we care."[1] This accords with Martin Luther's statement that because the heathen cannot see our faith, they ought to see our works. If our works show forth the Christ, he insisted, unbelievers may then hear our doctrine and, as a result, be converted.

Jesus' emphasis on loving deeds hardly justifies the conclusion that beliefs and personal faith are unimportant. Personal faith in Christ, not humanitarian concern, is the indispensable condition for salvation. Persons are accepted or rejected on the basis of their response to Jesus Christ. Nonetheless, the surest evidence of our life in Christ is love for the brethren (1 John 3:14) and a compassion shown in meeting actual human needs (1 John 3:17; Jas. 2:14-18). The rich grace of God reaches us in our sins and brings new life to us (Eph. 2:1-9). Salvation is a work of God in us; it is not "a result of works." Unfortunately, people sometimes leave the discussion at that point. To do so is to ignore a great truth: We are God's workmanship, "created in Christ Jesus for good works, which God prepared beforehand, that we should walk in them" (v. 10).

For the follower of Christ, loving acts in Christ's name are the natural fruit of faith. They flow out of a good heart, like delectable water flowing from a pure spring (Luke 6:45). Authentic faith leads to worthy works. Faith without works is dead. Keeping books on our acts may be pharisaical. Failure to act at all is non-Christian.

Notice the categories of human need which Jesus listed, and the concrete actions required to meet these needs. He put ministry down where people could handle it. He advocated immediate response, in practical deeds calculated to help the distressed. When persons are hungry, give them food, not advice or reprimands. Thirsty people need water, not merely a gospel tract or a lecture. Better still, we may provide help in digging wells, building dams, and devising irrigation systems. Naked persons must have adequate clothes suitable for the heat and cold. A lot of good wishes can be demoralizing unless accompanied by suitable raiment. The lonely stranger is helped by hospitality and friendship, not by pity and casual greetings (Heb. 13:2). Sick persons require proper medical attention, the touch of friendly hands, and visits that communicate love and encouragement. Prisoners are persons, guilty or innocent. They experience loneliness, guilt, fear, and emptiness. Persons who go to these societal outcasts with friendship, true compassion, and forgiving love must seem like angels to them.

Jesus could have extended the list of human needs from six to sixty! What about persons deprived of education, helpless victims of broken homes, individuals trapped in the poverty of the ghetto, or lives wasted by drugs and alcohol, or caught up in other demoralizing patterns of behavior. Love like that of Christ overlooks no category of need. Compassion such as He displayed toward others guides us into all kinds of helping ministries. No legalism should limit us to the six types of need mentioned in the parable (Matt. 25:35-36), but no callousness of soul should cause us to do less than the parable requires.

Authentic saints of God practice what they read in Scripture and find in Christ. They engage in unselfish services that benefit people who are hungry, distressed, sick, or economically deprived. The full extent of such gracious living often goes undetected until they have died and people are assessing their true worth.

This was true in the case of a quiet little woman called Frances Elizabeth Price, who lived and died in a rural community in western North Carolina. As people gathered to pay homage to this godly woman, they reflected on the kindly deeds she had done over the years. Their comments were like those of the wise man who portrayed the worthy woman (Prov. 31:10-27), or Luke's story of the noble Dorcas who was remembered for her good deeds (Acts 9:36-39). These are some of the things people noted about Mrs. Price:

"She loved her church and seldom missed a service."

"She practiced kindness and hospitality, and often had guests at the Sunday table."

"She was a good neighbor, always giving plants, vegetables, or other foodstuffs to persons in need."

"Once when we lost our milk cow, she gave us a heifer calf."

"We could never have gone to college but for Mother's hard work and sacrifice."

Listening in on all these comments from persons black or white, one came to the conclusion that life is best served and God is most honored by people who are honest, kindly, industrious, and self-forgetting. They pour their lives out in gracious ministries to persons.

Scripture, we say, tells us what God regards as important for people to believe and do. That being true, what we do *to* and *for* one another is frightfully important. For centuries the church has been preoccupied with doctrine, too frequently overlooking the ethical dimension of human responsibility. The twentieth century has not removed interest in theology, but it has brought the ethical demands of God to our attention. Those demands are found throughout the Bible (Ex. 20:1-17; Lev. 19; Deut. 5; Job 31; Ps. 15; Isa. 58; Amos 5:10-24; Matt. 5:1 to 7:29; Luke 10:25-37; Rom. 12:1 to 14:23; Jas. 1:27; 2:14-16).

Jesus' insistence on our meeting human need is therefore true to the mind of God. To ignore this responsibility is an act of disobedience, a denial of Christ, a failure to be truly human. Churches and individual Christians may pass fine resolutions and stress doctrinal orthodoxy. But these are no substitute for faithful ministry directed at the human miseries that confront us. "Passing by on the other side" keeps our skirts clean and our hands unsoiled. It also incurs the scorn of a world that sees the distance between our profession and our performance.

Talk shows generally devote themselves to mere talk, but

they do reveal the mind of the public. Recently a Nashville radio station, conducting such a talk show, carried the views of a person angry with Christians. "Christians and churches take the fun out of life. They are against gambling, even though the public wants it. They try to control the lives of other people. I think the Romans were right: Feed these folks to the lions!" Back of that man's angry view was the concept that churches should keep to themselves and not try to impact society. That is a view quite common in Russia and other Communist lands!

Marxist communism initially reacted to a corrupt church and a distorted gospel. The angry caller on the talk show might have been more positive about Christianity had he seen the great good Christians do in providing food, shelter, medical aid, and brotherly love. The early church won its way in a hostile world by its fidelity to Christ's love commandment and a courage born of faith in Him.

Should the Christian church turn works of mercy and healing over to the state? Some social philosophers may argue that Christians fulfill their stewardship through tax payments that support the federal government's social programs. All able citizens do share in the tax load that makes possible programs for human welfare. But the church can never push its responsibility off onto the shoulders of the state, any more than it can bear the entire burden of the nation's welfare. Churches lack the vast resources of the state. What we can do, however, we must do in caring for our own (1 Tim. 5:8). Thereby churches and individuals are true to Jesus' spirit, and they point the way for others to follow.

The Final Judgment Discloses the High Priority God Puts on Deeds Done for Others

Those deeds become the basis of judgment itself. Since judgment is the business of God, He determines the criteria for it.

God Alone Can Handle the Ultimate Separation of Persons

We are not good enough to sit in judgment of others. Our own lives are marked by sin and self-interest. Nor do we know enough to discern the motives and understand the actions of persons. In Palestine, the shepherd could easily separate white sheep from black goats. But human beings in their attitudes and behavior come in varying shades of gray. No one of us is equipped to divide persons into groups that bear labels marked good or evil. God alone is qualified to do that, for He possesses both the wisdom and the goodness to evaluate individuals. We ourselves are more like culprits who merit judgment (2 Cor. 5:10) than judges who can read human minds. Humility becomes us rather than a harsh judgmental stance.

Joaquin Miller expresses well that spirit of humility:

> In men whom men condemn as ill
> I find so much of goodness still,
> In men whom men pronounce divine
> I find so much of sin and blot,
> I do not dare to draw a line
> Between the two, where God has not.[2]

According to a Mississippi pastor, a church he knew did "draw a line," at least each Sunday morning when the people assembled for worship. An elderly man divided the congregation. He was well acquainted with the conduct patterns of the members. On the basis of that knowledge, he carefully and emphatically separated the sheep from the goats. When the people were settled in their proper places, the worship then commenced.

Who among us would attempt to divide a congregation like that? We would not, but Jesus can. He saw life's contrasting patterns. He spoke often of wheat and tares, light and darkness, broad and narrow ways, sheep and goats. Because He knows what is in persons (John 2:24-25), He can draw a line and issue decrees of judgment.

On what basis does Jesus pass judgment? Well, for one thing, He departs from the standards that we usually employ. The parable makes no mention of political or party ties. The standard of race fails to impress the Judge. People make so much of skin color; sometimes they use color as a basis of judging another human being. However, wealth and class cut no ice at the final judgment. Education is a symbol that most people prize. But the Judge never looks for persons with diplomas in their hands. Nor does He inquire about their church loyalties or mastery of doctrinal truth.

The Judge Tests Persons as to Their Deeds of Kindness Done to Persons in Need

Mind you, He does not discount the value of belief in sound doctrine. But belief must lead to behavior that ministers to persons. The most orthodox faith and the most precise theology are empty unless they lead us to works of love and mercy. Any religious position that causes us to ignore persons is a denial of Christ. God is not impressed with mere words or theological niceties.

Priests and Levites functioned well in the big Temple, but their conduct before a battered traveler along the roadside was heartless and shameful. In contrast, a man despised by Jewish religionists felt a deep compassion for the half-dead victim. Compassion led him to engage in a service that was eminently personal and practical (Luke 10:30-35). That Samaritan has for centuries symbolized genuine neighborly love. Jesus lifted him up as a model for all to follow (vv. 36-37).

The Eternal God who created and holds the universe together is vitally concerned about persons. He cares for each individual and is respecter of none (Acts 10:34). John Baillie, in *The Sense of the Presence of God,* insists that we must share this divine concern for people. We love God and our brother only as we hold these in relation to each other. "The way to God," Baillie declares, "passes through my relation to my neighbor, and the way to my neighbor passes through my relation to God."[3] One biblical writer, also named John, put it bluntly: "If someone says, " 'I love God,' and hates his brother, he is a liar; for the one who does not love his brother whom he has seen, cannot love God whom he has not seen" (1 John 4:20). Loving deeds toward God's children are good evidence of our relationship to Him.

Jesus Claims a Close Identification with the Poor, Disadvantaged, Needy People of Earth

This is clear, not only in the parable, but from the gospel records in general. Jesus had the habit of *seeing* people. His quick compassion led Him to help lonely persons like Zacchaeus, rejected women like Mary Magdalene, individuals sick in body or mind, poor people ground down by oppressive rulers. He was always on the side of the helpless. Is it any different today? He is close beside the diseased and distressed, the poor and forgotten members of society, the victims of war and famine, the wretched prisoner and the abused child. All these are objects of His love. They must be our concern as well.

The claim to follow Christ is thus substantiated by our ministry to human need. Listen to Jesus' words: "I was hungry . . . I was thirsty . . . I was a stranger . . . I was naked . . . I was sick . . . I was in prison . . . To the extent that you did it to one of these brothers of Mine, even the least of them, you did it to Me." Christ comes to us in others: in persons who are weak or insignificant, those most likely to be overlooked, despised, and neglected—in short, "the [very] least" among us. If we fail to see Him there, we are too blind to see Him anywhere.

After a decade of teaching in a respected theological seminary, I returned to the work of a pastor. When the initial excitement of that venture had subsided, I settled down to the frightfully busy routine of sermon building, meetings, membership recruitment, pastoral evangelism, and endless visitation. One busy day, I made the rounds of four hospitals to visit ailing church members. As I walked down the hallway to make my final visit, I found myself weary and full of self-pity. *Did I leave the seminary classroom,* I mused, *to become a hospital chaplain?* Then, in one of those moments rare to me, a light burst in my brain and a voice seemed to say, "I was sick, and you visited Me." Nothing so chastens a person as a reminder like that! Christ had been before me in every sick person that day, but I saw Him only in that last person I visited.

What Actions Are You Engaged in to Help Persons, and What Motivates You to Those Ministries?

Our humanitarian deeds can, of course, be rather empty if only pity or duty drives us, or if we perform them for the recognition or "emotional kick" they bring. God is honored when our services grow out of a heart that belongs to Christ. Surrounded by the hurts of humanity, Christians act out of love to do what each situation demands. Here is a widow, a retired nurse, who is going to a distant land to use her skill among a people desperate for such help. Christian men and women today are going with medical, dental, engineering, or agricultural skills to countries far removed to share their knowledge and gifts. One pastor in Rome, Georgia, describes a lay group known as "Carpenters for Christ" who use their expertise to assist in building churches and mission stations both here and abroad. These laymen find incredible joy in such building ventures. Why not? They are doing them as "unto the Lord."

Ministry to human need is not always dramatic and often goes unheralded. In most instances, it flows spontaneously and naturally out of a heart that Christ has touched. Goodness is "unconscious"; it keeps no records of deeds done, even seems unaware of ministries performed. Obviously, there is a place for planned ministry and development of strategies for meeting massive needs. But God's people seek no acclaim for their deeds, nor do they regard themselves too good to be wasted on the least and the lowest.

The Final Judgment Contains Some Surprising Verdicts

One group lauded by the Judge was surprised that their acts of mercy ministered to Christ Himself. "Lord, when did we minister to You in these ways?" Another group, not at all ignorant of the Master, had failed to be compassionate and caring toward others. They had failed to see the face of Jesus in human need. Tragically, they were blind to this omission. "Lord, when did we see You in dire need and fail to take care of You?"

Judgment Day has its surprises. But it has no time or place

for repentance. Its verdicts are irrevocable. Fortunately for us, God gives us this preview of things to come. The Judge posts the exam questions before the examination day. Wise persons, knowing the questions, will surely be at work on them now. The Judge who alone is able to separate persons in the judgment is able also to prepare us against that inevitable day.

The Church in Your House

Romans 16:5; 1 Corinthians 16:19; Philemon 2

In pioneer areas, some people know the meaning of the words "the church in your house." A house may serve both as home for a family and a congregation. The dwelling sometimes is designed with that dual function in mind. On Easter Sunday, 1981 my wife and I visited such a "house-church" in Weimea, Hawaii. Earlier that day, a small group had occupied the building for Bible study and worship. That afternoon, the gracious pastor and his family welcomed us into the part of the house where they lived.

Eventually, the growth of a congregation makes other arrangements necessary. But for months the house is both a meeting place and a home. What is it like to maintain a family under such circumstances? How are family members affected by periodic invasions of their privacy? Does enclosure within a household enhance the church's understanding of itself as a family, an intimate fellowship? Is the family's faith deepened by this exposure to God within the walls of its dwelling?

House-churches in the New Testament have been likened to modern cottage prayer meetings or weekly Bible study groups that meet in homes. The analogy is helpful, though the church is more than either. A church in the house brings together two institutions that are indispensable for human happiness and welfare. Each has its unique functions, but in the purpose of God they are allies, charged with the spiritual and moral well-being of humanity.

The House-Church Was Born of Necessity

Initially, the house-church was born of necessity. By nature the church is a fellowship of persons meeting occasionally for worship. This requires a meeting place. Even before Christians were denied the use of the Temple and the synagogue, they gathered in private homes for prayer and worship. "Breaking bread from house to house" is Luke's way of describing this practice (Acts 2:46). The house of Mary, John Mark's mother, was used for praise and prayer (Acts 12:12). Converts like Lydia and the Philippian jailer formed Christian life centers in their homes (Acts 16:13-15,25-34). Those homes, transformed by Christ, became launching pads for evangelistic work. In Troas, believers gathered in an upper room for the preaching of the gospel (Acts 20:7-12).

House-churches apparently existed in many cities. Some New Testament scholars note the size of the Jerusalem church and claim that it consisted of many small groups meeting in private homes. There was no building in the city large enough to accommodate the gathering of several hundred persons. Such a crowd would also have aroused the curiosity of Rome's peace-keeping force.

Outside Jerusalem also, the use of homes for worship and fellowship was commonplace. Church buildings as such appeared only in the third century. Our modern churches with their structures, furnishings, organizations, musical instruments, sound systems, parlors, and kitchens were unthinkable in the early centuries of Christianity. Christians met in private homes. Most of those houses were small and simply furnished. But they were dynamic "church life centers."

In the early years of the church, Christians frequently held their meetings at night. This was the most suitable time for members who belonged to the working classes (slaves and laborers) because they were occupied by day. Meetings were sometimes held in secret and the nighttime favored this. Rome was very wary of such gatherings. J. B. Lightfoot says the Roman government eventually came to recognize Christians as *collegia* or burial clubs and so allowed their meetings. Under this sort of protection, Christians gathered for religious purposes.[1] One may hazard the guess that those little bands of believers, not bound to structures and buildings as we are, were fully conscious of being God's people. The church in the private home brought the living presence of God into that household. It was an intimate fellowship.

House-churches, so some feel, are still viable methods of reaching people who are not enamored of institutional churches. Churches in large metropolitan areas, with dispersed members, have at times formed small cells or groups which meet periodically as integral parts of the main body. Multiple housing units, high-rise apartments, and isolated complexes with security guards challenge the contemporary church. The house-church or a small group working from within these complexes may offer hope for reaching people therein. What holds promise as a viable strategy for reaching people today was in the early Christian centuries a necessity for the church.

Paul pays tribute to three homes that housed church groups. Each could be viewed as "a household of the faith" (Gal. 6:10), or "the household of God" (Eph. 1:22-23; 2:19). Each was an *ekklēsia*, the people of God, the ones called out. In every sense of the word, those little congregations were true churches, marked by the presence of Christ Himself. For where the church gathers, He is present and that presence constitutes the church.

Each Family Can Be a House-Church

In a day when church buildings dot the whole landscape we may question that statement. What does it mean to have a church within the home?

The traditional pattern of the church is familiar enough. It involves people drawn away from their homes to designated houses of worship. The average congregation consists of many families or individuals. Each church has a number of performers (pastor, musicians, choir, ushers) and a large group of spectators whose participation is minimal.

No one would discount the importance of the traditional church and its place in contemporary society. Yet the home also becomes a little church when the gospel impacts the household. This church in the house then performs certain

vital functions as is evident in examples drawn from the New
Testament.

Evangelism

The first of these functions is evangelism. The New Testament gives five instances in which family members were converted and baptized (Acts 10:44-48; 16:15,30-34; 18:8; 1 Cor.
1:16). While the records are silent about the ages of those who
were baptized, the biblical emphasis is on faith in Christ as a
condition for salvation (Acts 16:31; Eph. 2:8). There is no scrip-
tural warrant for a proxy faith. Each person's response to
Christ calls for some understanding of sin and the need for
salvation.

Parents are in a strategic position to help their children
develop a sensitivity to sin and make a response to Christ. God
has placed on fathers and mothers the unique responsibility for
the spiritual welfare of their young. Family-centered evangelism, of course, may involve adult and youth, but the primary
focus here is on children in the home. While the church may
assist couples in their evangelistic task, no one can replace
them as spiritual guides within the family.

One indispensable aid in parental evangelism, according to
Professor William Hendricks, is a proper understanding of the
child in relation to divine grace. A theology of childhood certainly would relieve parents of unnatural fears for the child's
spiritual well-being. God does not destine small children to hell!
They are protected by His grace and brought in time to their
age of accountability. Along the way, children ask probing
questions about God, life, and death. Such questions are natural for inquisitive little minds, especially if they have been
exposed to biblical teachings. A child's awakening interest in
Jesus need not herald a readiness for salvation. Like other
interests, it affords parents those teachable moments when the
child is responsive to honest truth and simple answers.

In light of this, parents are enabled to keep down anxieties
and refrain from rushing small children into premature decisions for Christ and church membership. A couple once came
to me with their five-year-old daughter. The child had been

asking lots of questions, one of which was "When can I be
baptized?" They felt that the little girl was ready for a public
confession of faith, and were afraid to hold her back. "She
might die and go to hell," they said, "and it would be our fault."
Parents like that have usually heard about one or more conversions among preschool children. They need a biblical theology
of childhood.

Parental evangelism includes the nurturing of children in
the Christian faith. Converts within the family or the church
need positive teaching in the Bible and Christian doctrine. The
Christian life, after all, is more than an initial experience of
grace. In a sense, parents help disciple their children, concerned for their growth toward moral and spiritual maturity.
Each child is a distinct individual and deserves respect and
careful handling. "Train up a child in the way he should go,"
that is, according to his nature and need. Both by example and
by precept, parents seek to accomplish that goal. This nurturing function of the home will be discussed more fully in the
following section.

The Development of the Christian Life

The church in the home focuses on the development of the
Christian life. Aquila and Priscilla model that function. This
couple moved about a great deal: from Rome to Corinth to
Ephesus, then to Rome again. Wherever they went they seemed
to form a church in their house (Acts 18:18-26; Rom. 16:3-5; 1
Cor. 16:19). Their home provided hospitality, love, friendship,
and peace for lonely or distressed persons. The little congregations gathering in their home for worship and fellowship included notables like Paul and Apollos.

Aquila and Priscilla were laypersons, tentmakers by trade.
Their "other vocation," to use Trueblood's term, was the development of believers in the faith. They helped to equip the eloquent Apollos for the work of ministry (Acts 18:24-28). Paul had
such great confidence in them that he left the work at Ephesus
in their hands (Acts 18:18-21). They were gifted, it would seem,
in the development of believers.

Christian homes are committed to character building and

the development of social values. A home is a small community where persons learn how to live in relation to others, how to give and take, how to become human in the best sense of the word. Sociologists have long valued the family's place in the socialization of individuals. The breakdown of the family thus constitutes a great loss for children and youth. Social values must be acquired elsewhere or personality lacks the balance needed for wholesome living.

During World War II, the small son of a soldier developed emotional problems. This child's father, due to war's demands, was away from home during the son's early life. A skilled pediatrician detected the child's emotional disorders and attributed it to the absence of the father. Said he, "Every child needs two parents if he is to develop normally. God Almighty made it that way."

What the doctor said of that child is true of the home in general. We are socially developed within a family. It is there that we come to know the meaning of love and kindness. The home teaches morals and values. The church in the house introduces us to the essential meaning of maleness and femaleness, the tender care of persons, generosity as opposed to selfishness, and the significance of worship. A father who had taught his children how to pray became very emotional as he described the meaning of daily family worship for his household. He pointed to a four-year-old daughter as he said, "She never lets us forget that it's time to read the Bible and pray."

For me, a simple farmer with a third-grade education was my religious mentor. When I was a small boy, he challenged me to join him in reading through the Bible. That, for me, was the beginning of a lifetime of joy in reading, studying, and expounding the Bible. Father and I had conversations across the years concerning biblical texts and teachings. Near the end of his life, I went to visit him. He was sitting in his favorite rocking chair reading his favorite book. As always, he had some questions for his preacher son to answer. It was the last time we ever talked like that. A few months later, he suffered a stroke and was soon gone from us. Despite all my years of learning and study, my love and reverence for the Book never exceeded his. But my devotion to it began when he invited me to join him in reading through the Bible.

Forgiveness and Acceptance of Persons

The church in the house practices forgiveness and acceptance of persons. There was a church in the home of Philemon (Philem. 2). Philemon was a wealthy Christian who owed his spiritual life to Paul's witness. Onesimus, slave of Philemon, had run away from his owner and gone to Rome. There he had met Paul and through him found freedom in Christ.

The apostle's personal letter to Philemon contained a plea that he receive Onesimus back into the household, "no longer as a slave, but . . . a beloved brother . . . both in the flesh and in the Lord" (v. 16). Under Roman law, a master had unlimited power over a slave. A thief and a runaway like Onesimus could have been punished by death. Paul acted as a mediator working to bring about reconciliation, restitution, and forgiveness. Onesimus must return to his master; Philemon must show brotherly love and forgiveness. The church in Philemon's house would then gain a new member. Forgiving love would create a new situation as it always does.

Within the family, love and forgiveness form the proper environment for the development of members. Indeed, these qualities are indispensable due to the personality differences and conflict situations typical of most homes. Husbands and wives often run afoul of each other; parents and children have clashes; children fuss and fight among themselves. The small battles can develop into sharp conflicts, leading to open breaks. Maturity and patience are tested in most households.

Forgiveness sometimes requires one to forsake "rights" if the wrongdoer is to be restored to his or her place within the family. Philemon had to set aside his rights as a master in order to receive Onesimus back into his home. Onesimus, in turn, could not allow his newfound freedom in Christ to override his sense of responsibility toward his earthly master. Because they both had experienced God's love and forgiveness, they were able to love and forgive each other. Forgiveness removes barriers that keep persons apart. It ends the war and ushers in peace.

Forgiveness and love lead to the acceptance of persons. Not only Philemon and his family, but the church in his house, accepted a runaway slave as a brother. Any household or church may contain members whose self-righteous, pharisaical spirit causes them to turn away from the repentant prodigal. The refusal or the inability to forgive others, however, reflects upon one's ability to receive forgiveness (Matt. 6:15; 18:35). Where the forgiving spirit is present, families can resolve differences and consolidate interests. Love leads us to respect persons, accepting them as unique beings of worth, and enables us to handle conflicts when they arise.

Every home can be a church, for the church is a fellowship where Christ dwells. Those New Testament Christians who made up the house-churches remind us that home and church are allies. Both are God-given institutions. Both are committed to the spiritual welfare of persons. They share similar goals and experience similar joys. Halford Luccock has well said that "the Christian home has been the church's secret weapon in God's Holy War against evil."[2]

Is there a church in your house, dear friend?

Notes

Chapter 1

1. Adolf Deissmann, *Paul: A Study in Social and Religious History,* Harper Torchbooks (New York: Harper & Brothers, 1957), p. 132.

2. Thomas M. Lindsay, *Luther and the German Reformation* (Edinburgh: T. & T. Clark, 1935), p. 30.

3. George Buttrick, *So We Believe, So We Pray* (New York: Abingdon-Cokesbury, 1951), p. 88.

Chapter 2

1. Eduard Schweizer, *The Good News According to Mark* (Atlanta: John Knox Press, 1976), p. 24.

2. Henry Turlington, "Mark," *The Broadman Bible Commentary* (Nashville: Broadman Press, 1969), vol. 8, p. 350.

Chapter 3

1. Frank Stagg, *The Doctrine of Christ* (Nashville: Convention Press, 1984), p. 106.

2. *The Death of Christ* (Nashville: Broadman Press, 1978), pp. 125-135.

3. F. F. Bruce, *The Epistle to the Hebrews* (Grand Rapids: Wm. B. Eerdmans Publishing Co.), p. 154.

4. Grace Noll Crowell, "Some One Had Prayed," from *Christ and the Fine Arts* (New York: Harper & Bros., 1938), p. 684.

Chapter 4

1. James Leo Garrett, Jr., "Recovering My Priesthood," *Home Missions* (February, 1965), pp. 14-15.

2. Cyril Eastwood, *The Priesthood of All Believers* (Minneapolis: Augsburg Publishing House, 1962), p. 77.

3. John Dillenberger, ed., *Martin Luther: Selections from His Writings,* Anchor Books (Garden City: Doubleday & Co., 1961), pp. 345 *ff.*

4. A. T. Robertson, *Word Pictures in the New Testament* (Nashville: Sunday School Board of the Southern Baptist Convention, 1931), vol. 4, p. 402.

Chapter 5

1. H. Richard Niebuhr, *The Purpose of the Church and Its Ministry* (New York: Harper & Bros., 1956), pp. 79 *ff.*

Chapter 6

1. William Barclay, *The Master's Men* (Nashville: Abingdon Press, 1959), p. 89.

2. Ross Mackenzie, *The Word in Action* (Richmond: John Knox Press, 1973), p. 12.

Chapter 7

1. King James Version, *New American Standard Bible, New International Version,* and others opt for the reading given. *Revised Standard Version, The Good News Bible,* and some commentators prefer a different reading.

2. According to the Tennessee Department of Evangelism.

3. Maurice W. Fogle, *Christians Together* (St. Louis: Bethany Press, 1957), p. 21.

Chapter 8

1. J. B. Lightfoot, *St. Paul's Epistle to the Philippians* (Grand Rapids: Zondervan, 1976), p. 167.

2. Dale Moody, "Romans," *The Broadman Bible Commentary* (Nashville: Broadman Press, 1970), vol. 10, p. 154.

3. Article, "John Thompson: Complex Coach," *The Tennessean,* March 17, 1985.

4. D.S. Schaff, "Savonarola," *The New Schaff-Herzog Encyclopedia* (Grand Rapids: Baker Book House, 1950), vol. 10, p. 217.

Chapter 9

1. Charles R. Swindoll, *Compassion* (Waco: Word Books, 1984), p. 40.

2. *1,000 Quotable Poems* (Chicago: Willett, Clark & Co., 1937), vol. 2, p. 228.

3. *Sense of the Presence of God* (London: Oxford University Press, 1962), p. 37.

Chapter 10

1. J. B. Lightfoot, *Saint Paul's Epistles to the Colossians and to Philemon* (Grand Rapids: Zondervan, 1971), p. 243.

2. Halford E. Luccock, *More Preaching Values in the Epistles of Paul* (New York: Harper & Bros., 1961), vol. 2, p. 246.